D1765829

Quest
for the Absolute

Joseph Maréchal

Quest for the Absolute

The Philosophical Vision of
Joseph Maréchal

Anthony M. Matteo

NORTHERN ILLINOIS UNIVERSITY PRESS
DeKalb 1992

∞

© 1992 by Northern Illinois University Press

Published by the Northern Illinois University Press,

DeKalb, Illinois 60115

Manufactured in the United States using acid-free paper

Design by Julia Fauci

Library of Congress Cataloging-in-Publication Data

Matteo, Anthony M.

Quest for the absolute: the philosophical vision of Joseph

Marechal / Anthony M. Matteo.

p.   cm.

Includes bibliographical references.

ISBN 0–87580–165-X

1. Maréchal, Joseph, 1878–1944. I. Title.

B4165.M324M37   1992

199'.493—dc20   91–26367

Contents

Introduction

Joseph Maréchal was born in Charleroi, Belgium, on 1 July 1878 and entered the novitiate of the Society of Jesus in September 1895. Despite recurrent ill health, which plagued him from adolescence onwards, he gradually completed the rigorous regimen of intellectual and spiritual formation mandated by the Jesuit order. After studying philosophy, he took up the natural sciences and was awarded a doctorate in natural science, summa cum laude, from the University of Louvain in 1905. Maréchal believed that a grounding in natural science helped guard against what he termed *"l'auto-suggestion métaphysique."*

After further theological study, Maréchal was ordained in 1908. In 1910 he began to offer courses in biology and psychology at the Jesuit scholasticate in Louvain. In 1911 he went to Germany to study experimental psychology and psychotherapy and visited such luminaries as Wilhelm Wundt and Wolfgang Köhler. At the start of World War I in 1914, Maréchal was sent with his Jesuit students to England, where he began to instruct them in philosophy. During this year he began work on what was to become his magnum opus, *Le Point de Départ de la Métaphysique: Leçons sur le Développement Historique et Théorique du Problème de la Connaissance.*

Maréchal returned to Belgium in 1915 and thereupon began his most prolific period of writing, which lasted until 1935. His chief works were a two-volume study of religious psychology and Christian and comparative mysticism, *Etudes sur la Psychologie des Mystiques*, and the five volumes of his masterful *Le Point de Départ de la Métaphysique*. The first three volumes of the latter were published in quick succession in 1922–23. Volume one, *De l'Antiquité à la fin du Moyen Age: La Critique Ancienne de la Connaissance*, traces the rise and fall of the Aristotelian-Thomistic synthesis. Volume two, *Le Conflit du Rationalisme et de l'Empirisme dans la Philosophie Moderne avant Kant*, recounts the ongoing dispute between rationalists and empiricists in pre-Kantian modern philosophy. In volume three, *La Critique de Kant*, Maréchal offers what is arguably the first balanced and fair appraisal of Kant's work by a Catholic scholar.

Although by 1923 the more phobic and virulent aspects of the anti-modernist crisis in Catholicism at the turn of the century had faded, Maréchal's largely favorable reading of Kant was still held in suspicion in some quarters. Thus, he moved directly to reworking and publishing (1926) volume five of *Le Point de Départ, Le Thomisme devant la Philosophie Critique*, to demonstrate the orthodoxy of his philosophical project. Volume four, *Le Système Idéaliste chez Kant et les Postkantiens*, was published posthumously in 1947 from manuscripts left by Maréchal.

Maréchal himself was an epistemological realist in the tradition of Aquinas. His most fervent intellectual aspiration was to rejuvenate that tradition by demonstrating its applicability and importance to the modern or post-Kantian philosophical milieu. This is the leitmotif of his study of the history of Western philosophy and of his intensive critical dialogue with Kant and post-Kantian idealism. Maréchal attempts to show that we must assume, like Aristotle and Aquinas, that our senses and intellectual faculties operate in a coordinated and complementary fashion if we are to achieve a coherent theory of knowledge. The history of Western philosophy, he contends, offers pronounced evidence that, when thinkers stray from this central tenet of Aristotelian and Thomistic epistemology, what they produce are idealist or empiricist caricatures of cognition.

In Maréchal's view, Kant implicitly grasped the necessity of presenting a harmonious account of the workings of sensation and intellection, but was barred from returning to a full-bodied realism by his overly static conception of the workings of human understanding in its quest for knowledge. Maréchal seeks to show that, once the dynamic nature of intellectual striving is recognized, then Kant's Copernican revolution in philosophy need not eventuate in Kant's own critical idealism, let alone nineteenth-century absolute idealism or twentieth-century agnosticism. Maréchal's daring claim is that, even beginning with a subjective starting point (our own content of consciousness) and employing transcendental method, the necessity of objective affirmation or epistemological realism will become manifest.

Since his death in 1944, Maréchal's work has inspired a number of eminent Catholic thinkers. It offers a viable defense of the philosophical realism inherited from the scholastic tradition that does not entail wholesale rejection of the modern "turn to the subject" as a point of departure for philosophical speculation. In this respect, Maréchal's work presents a marked contrast to the neo-Thomist program that wielded such influence in Catholic circles from the mid-nineteenth century onward, and whose primary posture vis-à-vis modern philosophical movements was highly defensive and apologetic in character. As Gerald McCool writes: "The general approach of the neo-Thomists was to argue that all the modern systems were intrinsically unsatisfactory. The adverb was all important. For, if the systems were intrinsically unsatisfactory, they could not be corrected from within; they would have to be replaced."[1]

Clearly, if one perceives the position of one's intellectual adversaries as inherently flawed, there is little if any incentive to initiate or sustain an effective dialogue, so that an open airing and possible resolution of conflicting claims might be achieved. Not surprisingly, then, the apologetic aims of the neo-Thomist program, backed by the full institutional support of the Vatican and Roman Curia, generated a "citadel mentality" that had a chilling effect on Catholic intellectual life well into the first half of this century.

Maréchal's work marks a definite foray outside the Catholic citadel. He succeeded in laying the groundwork for a rapprochement between the thought of Aquinas and the transcendental analysis inaugurated by Kant. Maréchal's goal was a creative integration of the ontological approach to knowledge of the Aristotelian-Thomistic tradition and the transcendental approach of Kantian criticism.

Maréchal's efforts resulted in an infusion of fresh air inside the Catholic citadel. His Transcendental Thomism had a formative influence on the development of the so-called New

Theology, as well as on the work of Karl Rahner and Bernard Lonergan, the two most notable Catholic thinkers of the second half of the twentieth century.

In perhaps his most lasting contribution to Catholic intellectual life, Maréchal showed Catholic thinkers that they could maintain their allegiance to the spirit of St. Thomas Aquinas yet still engage in a critical and open conversation with modern intellectual movements—that, in fact, the spirit of Aquinas encouraged just such an endeavor. As McCool points out, this ironically turned the nineteenth-century neo-Thomist appropriation of Aquinas right on its head.

> And, as if to heighten the irony, the New Theologians performed their act of unfilial betrayal by exploiting the philosophic potentialities of the weapon their ancestors had used to undermine the epistemology and metaphysics on which their opponents' modern theologies were built. This weapon was St. Thomas' metaphysics of man and being which the metaphysics of knowledge required.[2]

Regrettably, Maréchal's own writings are little known and have had scant influence outside the realm of Catholic scholars. However, in the course of this work, I will attempt to indicate how his insights might be fruitfully related to the contemporary discussions now occupying the broader philosophical community. His work appears particularly apropos of the current debate centering on the foundations of rationality and the renewed controversy surrounding cognitive relativism.

Maréchal's extensive historical propaedeutic—wherein he insightfully surveys the ongoing struggle between empiricist and rationalist strains in Western thought since the late Middle Ages—provides us with an informed vantage point from which to ponder the current debates over rationality and relativism. His historical findings suggest that only an account of cognition which respects the primal complementarity of our senses and intellectual capacities can hope to clarify, rather than obscure, the actual workings of our mental life. He reminds us that we must be attentive to the distinction between the content of thought and the activity of thinking by which that content is generated. We must not only cast the light of reflection on the myriad theoretical constructs by which human beings have sought to comprehend their world, but also on the drive toward ever greater levels of intelligibility that continually impels them to form, criticize, and reformulate such constructs. Reflection on this activity, drive, or pure desire to know reveals that a commitment to the principle of intelligibility is not merely optional, but represents a necessary a priori condition for the possibility of thought itself. Furthermore, Maréchal contends, such reflection reveals that we must envision every individual attempt to understand, or render intelligible, some aspect of the universe against the backdrop of the overarching human quest for complete knowledge or total intelligibility. In short, the quest for God, the absolute being, whose existence finally renders the relative or contingent beings of our experience intelligible, is the ultimate animating force underlying all our cognitive efforts.

Although tomes have been written on the work of Maréchal's prominent intellectual heirs, such as Karl Rahner and Bernard Lonergan, remarkably, there is no clear, complete, and readable exposition of Maréchal's thought currently available. This book represents an effort to respond to that lacuna in scholarship. As far as my own capacities permit, I have tried to produce a volume that will be accessible not only to professional philosophers, but to anyone with a general knowledge of, and interest in, the history of Western philosophy and what it has to teach us about our current philosophical and cultural conundrums. Each reader will have to judge to what extent the attempt has been successful.

Quest
for the Absolute

CHAPTER ONE

The Rise and Fall of the Aristotelian-Thomistic Synthesis

I n the introduction to the first volume of *Le Point de Départ de la Métaphysique* (hereafter referred to as *Le Point de Départ*), Joseph Maréchal sets forth the major question to be elucidated throughout the course of his five-volume opus: "If metaphysics is to be possible, it necessarily has an absolute objective affirmation as its point of departure: in our content of consciousness do we meet such an affirmation surrounded by all the guarantees demanded by the most exacting critique?"[1]

At issue for Maréchal is whether our knowledge is indeed a direct knowledge of the world or merely an awareness of our own subjective representations, whose relations to the external world are at best problematic. He is not, however, calling for a return to the misguided *quaestio de ponte*, that phantom quest in post-Cartesian philosophy for a way to reunite thinking beings (*res cogitans*) and material reality (*res extensa*) after Descartes had split them asunder. If our starting point in metaphysics is an exclusive analysis of the purely subjective content of consciousness, then a gap is created between our conceptions (our mind or brain states) and the things to which they supposedly refer, which no amount of philosophical finesse can successfully bridge. Hence, metaphysics must be grounded in a *direct* knowledge of the world or, to put the issue in scholastic terms, our concepts must be vehicles by which we come to know the world (*id quo intelligitur*), and not themselves the sole object of knowledge (*id quod intelligitur*). "If we attain metaphysical truth, it will be, in the final analysis, by the light of immediate objective evidence."[2]

This much could have been written by a conservative nineteenth-century Scholastic such as Joseph Kleutgen. In his scathing critique of modern philosophy, *Philosophie der Neuzeit,* Kleutgen lashes out at the subjectivist turn in Western philosophy since Descartes. He sees this move as tending toward phenomenalism and relativism, both of which are ultimately destructive of a coherent metaphysical vision.[3] Maréchal, for his part, believes that simply raising the specter of the demise of metaphysics will have little impact on those who see its downfall as the inevitable result of the rigorous critique of knowledge that has been the hallmark of modern philosophy. An agnostic epistemology that leads to relativism or pragmatism may fly in the face of our apparent tendency to affirm the objective nature of our knowledge but, in the light of modern philosophical research, such a tendency is seen by many as naive and outdated.

Hence, if we are to vindicate the claims of philosophical realism, Maréchal holds that we must do more than dogmatically assert the necessity of objective affirmation. Rather, we must employ critical analysis to demonstrate the erroneous nature of the various forms of philosophical relativism. We must show that such positions rest upon an inherent contradiction. Only then can we claim a theoretical victory. In Maréchal's words, "metaphysical affirmation must don a theoretical and not only a moral or practical necessity if it is to oppose itself victoriously to relativism."[4] Thus Maréchal sets himself apart, at the very outset, from dogmatic, realist assertions on the one hand, and, on the other, from "soft" attempts to justify metaphysical claims after the fashion of a "philosophy as if" or a pragmatically based "will to believe." If his efforts to defend realism are to succeed, he wants the issue to be decided by a process of reasoning as exacting as that employed by the most tough-minded of his adversaries.

Maréchal initiates this process by seeking to unearth the roots of relativism in both ancient and medieval philosophy.

Two fundamental questions serve as guides in this complex investigation:

1. Since the absolute affirmation of the object, that is, the metaphysical affirmation, represents the natural attitude of the human mind, how did some philosophers reach the point where they demanded a critical justification of the primordial affirmation? In other words, how could the critical problem of knowledge originate?
2. To what extent is such a justification possible? In other words, is there a solution to the critical problem of knowledge.[5]

Plaguing doubts about the objectivity of our knowledge did not simply burst onto the scene with modern philosophy. Maréchal seeks to portray such doubts as emerging from deep intellectual currents in the history of Western thought.

The Rise of Skepticism

The religious myths and ancient poetic cosmogonies of Greek civilization display a rapturous fascination with the genesis and wondrous workings of the natural order. The Ionian philosophers, who were the initiators of rational speculation among the Greeks, were likewise preoccupied with cosmological considerations. These early thinkers simply did not doubt the objectivity of their affirmations about the universe. Their realism was "dogmatic," in that critical epistemological questions were not raised. Of this inceptive phase of Western philosophy Maréchal writes:

> The absolute value of objective affirmation was still in no way placed in doubt. The affirmation itself was connected with the entire content of thought furnished by experience, under the sole caution of a certain organization of the content. Philosophy thus followed without much effort the twofold natural penchant of the mind to affirm and to unify.[6]

These philosophical pioneers assumed the validity of the natural or spontaneous tendency toward realist affirmation. Based on this assumption, they sought a unified vision of the universe in their quest for the primal element or elements out of which all else was constructed. But the very pursuit of an ever more comprehensive unity underlying the multiplicity of the universe resulted in the eventual shattering of the Edenic period of Ionian speculation. When philosophy set upon "being" as the primal and universal building block of metaphysical unity, dogmatic realism faced its first substantial challenge.

What was the true nature of "being?" Simple observation of the universe did not at that time seem to yield a definitive answer. Heraclitus held that multiplicity and change were universal and the apparent stability of things was illusory. All was in a state of continual "becoming"! Parmenides enunciated the opposite view. "Being" was one and immovable, and thus change was mere appearance. Reason had fallen into a paradox. It did not seem possible to affirm the reality of stability or change without consigning its opposite to the realm of illusion. Competing and contradictory philosophical schools arose and, thereby, the ground was prepared for the first major challenge to the congenitally realist bent of Greek thought, namely, the rise of the skeptical Sophists.

Maréchal asserts that the root of Sophistic skepticism was the denial of the first principle of rational thought and discourse, the principle of identity. If this fundamental principle is not operative, then judgment is mired in insurmountable uncertainty and a realist metaphysical stance is rendered senseless.

According to Maréchal, the Aristotelian reply to skepticism provides the essential refutation of that philosophical position. One cannot, strictly speaking, give a demonstration of the principle of identity for, precisely as first principle, it is presupposed in all logical deductions.[7] One can, however, point out that the skeptic is enmeshed in a living contradiction. Although it is theoretically possible for the skeptic to resist the tendency toward objective affirmation on the grounds that sufficient cognitive warrants for such an affirmation are not present, at the practical level of everyday existence such a stance is not possible. "In the order of ends objective affirmation is inevitable."[8] One may adopt a theoretical attitude of detachment vis-à-vis the "truth question," but, at the concrete level of human existence, decisions in this regard are unavoidable.

Human existence is inherently goal-oriented. Our pursuit of one objective rather than another rests on our personal commitment, however tentative, to the accuracy of our analysis of the situation at hand. Clearly, a consistent and total policy of suspending judgment (*epoche*) in relation to truth would result in an absurd state of paralysis. Hence, one who espouses a position of total skepticism is a living contradiction, for his daily acts belie his stated theoretical position.

Maréchal describes the contradictory posture of the skeptic as follows: "If he contents himself with a passive attitude, he, consciously or unconsciously, is being untrue to life which ineluctably pushes him forward along the path of affirmation and action: each of his desires or his acts belies his theoretical attitude." [9]

In addition, Maréchal points out that the very attempt of the skeptic to abstain from judgment and affirmation is *itself* an act of affirmation (*nolo velle est volo nolle*). Drawing at this point on the work of Maurice Blondel, he asserts that the mind is impelled by a natural and persistent tendency toward affirmation: "To withstand this inner and permanent impulsion is not the same as to yield to complete passivity, to an absolute lack of activity; it implies rather a strong reaction against oneself, deriving from a precise and firm decision: it means breaking the affirmative mood of the intellect by means of an affirmation which is even more basic and more ruthless." [10]

Furthermore, the attempt to avoid affirmation does not result in the negation of all possible knowledge; such a posture on the part of the skeptic would entail complete silence as its necessary correlate. Rather, it is the skeptic's way of insisting on the probity of his own beliefs. [11]

Thus, in Maréchal's analysis, the skeptic emerges as an intellectual narcissist who is unwilling to yield to the mind's natural urge to transcend itself in the pursuit of a truth to which it is obliged to conform. The skeptical posture is thereby unmasked as an inconsistent attempt to justify a narrow dogmatism of self-assertion behind the veil of critical severity. In this context, Maréchal quotes Blondel with approval:

When the dilettante glides between the stone fingers of all idols, he does so because he accepts some other worship, self-worship: as he looks down on everything from the height of Sirius, everything seems so narrow and petty to him, everything except the love of one being, of *himself*. . . . Thus the very fact of not willing conceals a subjective end. Not to will anything means to refuse oneself to every object in order to keep oneself entirely to oneself, in order to reject every gift, every devotion, every abnegation.[12]

A dose of skepticism toward particular theories or systems of explanation is an effective antidote to naive credulity and our ever-present tendency to absolutize partial perspectives. But a skepticism that calls into question the mind's very capacity to arrive at insights into the actual truth of the matter would be lethal to rational investigation. Maréchal wishes to point out that such a radical skepticism is, in fact, unlivable. Skeptics pride themselves on their intelligence and judiciousness, but they have strong preferences that reveal their latent affirmation of the way the world actually is. Why, then, do they cling theoretically to a position that, practically speaking, is untenable? Maréchal agrees with Blondel that to proclaim all things doubtful, except one's own doubts, amounts to an intellectual tour de force. The unanalyzed underside of the radical skeptic's position is his desire to rationalize the ultimate dogmatism, namely, *La verité c'est moi!*

Aristotle's Response—A Coherent Theory of Knowledge

Although, to Maréchal, the skeptical posture of the ancient Sophists was insupportable, their forceful challenge compelled Greek metaphysical speculation to refine its "realist" foundations by explicating more fully the elements of the cognitive process. In short, the Sophists were instrumental in precipitating the first "critical" turn in the Western philosophical tradition. As a result, writes Maréchal,

> it was necessary not only to perfect and render coherent the metaphysics of the "object" (in a restricted sense); not only to develop the metaphysics of the human "subject," considered in itself as a substance, but also to make room, in the context of metaphysical affirmation, for that relation of subject to object that we perceive each time that we are aware of knowing.[13]

The antinomy of being and becoming (the one and the many) shattered the dogmatic-realist slumber of ancient Greek thought. Securing the principle of identity and the necessity of affirmation against the corrosive effects of skepticism represented only a partial rehabilitation of the foundations of the cognitive process. What was also required was a critical and coherent analysis of both poles of this process: the knowing subject and the object known. Only then could the multiplicity and change revealed through sense experience be harmonized with the unity and stability that were the fruit of intellectual insight. Although Maréchal recognizes Socrates and Plato as forerunners in this task, he credits Aristotle with having accomplished it with full comprehension and clarity.

Like his mentor Plato, Aristotle held that true scientific knowledge is knowledge of universals. Intelligibility cannot be explained by the welter and flux of particulars, but requires some unifying and stabilizing foundation. However, unlike Plato, Aristotle did not seek that foundation in the transcendent realm of Ideas (*Eidos*) but within the sensible realm of experience itself.

In trying to resolve the antinomy of the one and the many Plato had set up two distinct realms, the intelligible and the sensible, linked only by the vague and tenuous notions of participation and imitation. The true lover of wisdom had to break away from the shadowy world of sense experience—the world of becoming—in order to rise to pure contemplation of the being of intelligible objects, that is, transcendent ideas. Plato's treatment of the sensible and intelligible components of the cognitive process, in which the former is definitely subordinated to the latter, resulted in a depreciation of the sensible and empirical level of experience. Once the highly problematic, artificial nature of Plato's notions of participation and imitation is exposed, the sensible and intelligible elements of knowledge still appear to be hopelessly at odds, and thus the original antinomy is not really overcome.

Aristotle realized that this apparent contradiction could be surmounted only if the compatibility or complementarity of the sensible and the intelligible could be demonstrated. To Maréchal, the guiding question of Aristotle's treatment of this issue was: "How is this interpenetration of the sensible and the intelligible conceivable?"[14]

Aristotle taught that the universal is immanent in the particular. All sensible objects are composed of matter and form. Form is not one component among others, but it is the "essence" of a thing, that which makes it what it is. Matter is the substrate or matrix in which form is actualized. These forms or immanent ideas are *only* to be found in particular, sensible objects. They have no transcendent or separate existence. They represent the foundation in sensible objects of the universal concepts that make reality intelligible. As Maréchal puts it, "the universal concept no longer results from an ontological intuition of subsistent ideas . . . it derives its origin from sensible things; in them we actually discover the intelligible."[15]

Furthermore, form is the basis of the unity of species (e.g., "man" or "horse") that we perceive in the world. As such, it is not restricted to any particular member of the species in question. "Form of itself, in its species, is unlimited as the Scholastics would later say."[16] Matter is the individualizing element that marks off one particular member of a species from another.

Our minds have no direct, intuitive access to forms or essences. Aristotle teaches that as a result of the contact between our senses and a sensible object we acquire a concrete mental image of that object. Then the active intellect abstracts the form by dematerializing the concrete image. This form is then impressed on the passive intellect and the result is the universal concept in its proper sense.

Maréchal holds that Aristotle's doctrine of universals and theory of abstraction mark a "critical" step forward for Greek epistemology. They demonstrate that our conceptual knowledge cannot naively be construed as a simple mirroring of external reality.

> The epistemological result is the statement, certainly new at the time, that the concept, while representing real objects, is not purely and simply a duplicate of reality . . . . That amounts to saying that the essence does not exist in things with the mode of universality that it takes on in the abstractive understanding. As a result, the necessary affirmation of the object or our concepts must be "critical"; it must discern in each concept, as the Scholastics would latter express it, that which is really signified (*quod significatur*) and the abstract mode of representation (*modus repraesentandi*), in other words, the participation of the object and the subject in the objective concept.[17]

In this view, our universal concepts do indeed put us in contact with external reality. Thus, a concept is a means to an end (*id quo*) and not an end in itself (*id quod intelligitur*). But concepts are a result of an intricate intellectual process that is set in motion by the encounter of our senses and intellect with the external world. This process must be critically analyzed and fully inventoried if knowledge is to be validated in the face of skeptical attack. In Aristotle's view, the quest for knowledge is a markedly human enterprise that seeks intelligible structures within the vast empirical data presented to the senses. We have no other access to the "real" save through the abstraction of intelligible forms from sensible images. We are not privy to mystical insights into the nature of things that somehow circumvent the normal functioning of the intellect.

Maréchal calls Aristotle's solution to the dilemma of the one and the many in ancient philosophy a "mitigation of the realism of the understanding."[18] Unlike Plato's approach, Aristotle's does not assume that our concepts simply mirror a transcendent realm of ideas. Aristotle seeks to justify the objectivity of our intellectual operations without reliance on what Maréchal calls "ontologist audacity" (*hardiesses ontologistes*): namely, the presupposition that our minds can make direct contact with a transempirical order.[19]

In Maréchal's view, Aristotle is the father of critical realism in the West. He not only successfully rebutted the Sophists, but also moved Western thought beyond the epistemological naïveté that is inherent in Plato's idealism and that, ironically, bedevils empiricism. Both assume that knowledge can be understood on a simple observational model.

In this context, the following remarks of Bernard Lonergan are helpful: "For man observes, understands and judges, but he fancies that what he knows in judgment is not known in judgment and does not suppose an exercise of understanding but simply is attained by taking a good look at the 'real' that is 'already out there now.'"[20]

Platonic thought posits a kind of "eye of the soul," which directly intuits objective universals in their transcendent purity. Not surprisingly, it so denigrates the sensible realm as to render the contribution of the senses negligible, if not a definite hindrance to the attainment of true knowledge. Empiricists, on the other hand, appeal to pure sense experience as the firm foundation of knowledge. But sense data, no matter how

carefully culled, are not equivalent to knowledge, which presupposes the processing and organization of raw sense data by
an intelligent agent.

Lonergan goes on to explain: "Experience is only the first
level of knowing; it presents the matter to be known. Understanding is only the second level of knowing; it defines the
matter to be known. Knowing reaches a complete increment
only with the judgment, only when the merely experienced has
been thought and the merely thought has been affirmed."[21]

Maréchal holds that Aristotle gives a critical analysis and explication of the knowledge we actually possess, while avoiding
the above extremes. Here, Maréchal echoes a theme that will
resonate throughout his writings: namely, that Aristotle's
metaphysical system, especially as refined by Aquinas, is based
on a critical foundation that can withstand attacks from both
empiricist and idealist perspectives.

Maréchal affirms that the validity of the first principle,
namely, the principle of identity, implies an absolute affirmation of "being," and the relegation of "nothingness" to the status of an illusory pseudoconcept. According to this principle,
to "be" is to be self-identical. "Not being" is always relative to,
or dependent on, a prior conception of "being." To conceive the
"not being" of A implies a prior conception of its "being."
Hence pure nonbeing or nothingness is unthinkable.

In addition, the principle of identity serves as an organizing
principle for our content of consciousness. Lacking such a principle, all would indeed be relative and unstable. In Maréchal's
words: "Every content of consciousness, by the very fact that it
is ruled by the first principle, is referred to the absolute order of
being: a mere relativity of the content of consciousness would
contradict the first principle."[22]

Hence, the first principle implies some form of stability and
unity in the order of being and rules out pure variability and
becoming. Aristotle thus seems to side with Parmenides
against Heraclitus as to the true nature of reality. But Parmenides feels it necessary to relegate multiplicity and change,
which are evident to the senses, to the status of illusory appearance in order to preserve the unity and intelligibility of being.
He can only conceive change or becoming as a passage from
nonbeing to being, which is unthinkable. Thus, Parmenides

concludes, what exists "remains the same, in the same . . . held fast by the power of necessity."[23]

Maréchal indicates that the acceptance of the principle of identity, and the concomitant conviction as to the unity and intelligibility of being, does not necessarily entail a Parmenidian philosophical monism. From the static point of view of Parmenides, "becoming," in the sense of a dynamic admixture of being and nonbeing, would of course be unintelligible.

Aristotle sought to explicate just such a dynamic understanding of "being" in a way that would do justice to the evidence of "change" or "becoming" given by the senses, without sacrificing the unity of being demanded by the principle of identity. Thus, he enunciated his doctrine of being in terms of act and potency. Aristotle did not interpret "becoming" as a passage from pure nonbeing to being. Understood in that light, it is indeed unthinkable. Rather, he described each individual existent as a combination of *relative* being and nonbeing, that is, of act (*entelecheia*) and potency (*dynamis*).[24]

The upshot of the Aristotelian doctrine is that "becoming" is neither impossible nor chaotic. It is not the case that A, which is completely and utterly not B, suddenly becomes B. The conditions necessary to become B must pre-exist in A if A is ever to become B. In Aristotelian language, A is in potency to B. Furthermore, the passage from potency to act requires the intervention of an agent already in act. Hence, actuality is ontologically prior to potency. In Aristotle's view, change or becoming is not the result of mere chance or mechanical necessity. With his doctrine of final causality he envisions change as purposeful and directed.[25] Appraising Aristotle's doctrine of act and potency, Maréchal writes:

> Aristotle says that all becoming proceeds from an act which is its moving principle and tends toward an act which it completes itself. . . . The totality of becoming, or becoming as such, thus necessarily develops between a universal principle, a "first mover" which is pure Act and an absolutely final end which is equally pure Act.[26]

Thus, to be coherent, the Aristotelian system requires a prime mover which is both beginning and end (*terminus a quo* and *terminus ad quem*) of the universal process of becoming or change. Aristotle describes the prime mover as pure Act with no taint of potency, whose attractive power is the cause and end of all movement in the cosmos.[27]

Although Aristotle's world consists of particular beings in a constant state of movement at the physical level, these particulars are rooted in the stability of unchanging metaphysical essences that ultimately make the particulars what they are. These essences are the foundation of our universal concepts and thus we can be certain of a correspondence between the logical and ontological orders. But can we, in our present context, fully share in this brand of Aristotelian certainty? Marjorie Grene points out that perhaps Aristotle's critical realism is not "critical" enough for our age:

> Everything in the world rests, for Aristotle, on the necessity of eternal, intelligible first things which could not be other than they are. . . . For us, on the contrary, the ground beyond which we cannot penetrate is the ultimate "that," the certainty of the non-necessary, of the facticity in which and through which we have our being and our contact with being. The unity of mind and object, which comes to rest forever in Aristotelian *nous*, for us is forever in tension. Contingency is never totally absorbed into significance: significance may always come to be reread, new visions, however compelling they once were, may let the old slip into the mere contingency of half-truth, falsehood, absurdity.[28]

Aristotle's perspective may have been sufficiently acute to lift naive realism to a higher, more sophisticated level, so as to cope with ancient skepticism. Nonetheless, it presupposes a level of constancy in the universe that we, who live in an intellectual milieu where historicist analysis and talk of incommensurable scientific paradigms have become commonplace, may be unable to accept.

In chapter 5, we shall assess Maréchal's claim that a fundamentally Aristotelian approach to epistemology and metaphysics can be adjusted to offer a defense of realism in the light of modern concerns.[29] For now, let us turn to what Maréchal has to say about the fate of Aristotle's insights in the Middle Ages.

Thomas Aquinas—The Recovery of Aristotelian Realism

When Europe emerged from the Dark Ages, a period in which critical philosophical activity in the West had lapsed into all but a moribund state, the subject of universals became a central concern of philosophers. Early medieval thinkers tried to resolve the dilemma surrounding this issue, but they were constrained to labor without the complete texts of the great masters of Greek antiquity. Even those texts that they did possess were in a confused state. Hence, it is not surprising that their speculations lack the rigor and sophistication of Aristotle's discussion of universals. Maréchal describes this period in the following manner:

> To tell the truth, during this entire period of groping, which leads from the ninth century to the end of the twelfth, it is not, properly speaking, a question of well-defined realism, conceptualism or nominalism. It is rather a phase of oscillating progression toward a unique terminal point of equilibrium, that of renewed Aristotelian realism. True nominalism, conscious of itself, does not arise until later at the decline of the Middle Ages.[30]

It was not until the reintroduction of the entire Aristotelian corpus into Europe in the twelfth century that Western philosophy could again treat epistemological and metaphysical questions, such as the status of universals, with requisite critical insight. By now a central tenet of Maréchal's reading of Western thought should be evident: namely, Aristotle's epistemological and metaphysical insights represent a balanced foundation for sound philosophical speculation. For Maréchal, Aristotle's guidance enables us to navigate successfully between the Scylla of naive or excessive realism, leading to pantheism and the Charybdis of nominalism, finally ending in skepticism. Repeatedly throughout *Le Point de Départ*, we find Maréchal asserting that, when philosophers in the West stray from a basically Aristotelian course, they become embroiled in intractable intellectual conundrums, from which they can only emerge by distorting some vital aspect of human cognitive experience.

A medieval thinker who did not so stray was, of course, Thomas Aquinas. Maréchal commends him for having appropriated Aristotelian principles in all their profundity and complexity. Like Aristotle, Aquinas asserts that the knowledge we actually possess is the result of an intimate collaboration of sense and intellect. He also accepts the Aristotelian distinction, fundamental to a critical realism, between the *modus intellectus* and the *modus rei*:

> For it is quite true that the mode of understanding, in one who understands, is not the same as the mode of a thing in being, since the thing understood is immaterially in the one who understands, according to the mode of the intellect, and not materially, according to the mode of a material thing.[31]

This distinction implies that one must precisely differentiate between the object as such and the object as known. In this context, Maréchal writes:

> Realism must be critical. There should be no indistinct affirmation without cognizance of the entire context of the mind. In order to be legitimate—and not to run into contradiction sooner or later—affirmation must disengage its object from the subjective mode in which it is enclosed; because *modus intellectus non est necessarie modus rei*. The realism of Saint Thomas as well as the realism of Aristotle demand a *critique of the object as thought*.[32]

But if we accept this distinction, must we not abandon all hope of justifying metaphysical realism? How, in this view, can we be assured that our conceptual knowledge of the world through universals (*modus intellectus*) is truly knowledge of the world itself and not merely a subjective account of our own (or our culture's) internal experience? To frame the matter in Kantian and contemporary terms: Once we admit that our knowledge is mediated by the categories of our human understanding or the confines of our conceptual scheme, how can the classical realist definition of truth as a correspondence (*adaequatio*) between thought and reality be warranted?

In his own historical context, Aquinas sought to defend the objective nature of our knowledge by insisting that our universal concepts are not, in the first place, what is known but the means by which we come to know the individual beings, including ourselves, that make up the world. In good Aristotelian fashion he teaches that the process of abstraction performed by the active intellect "dematerializes" and thus "deindividualizes" the sensible image or phantasm of the individual object and so captures its metaphysical essence (*quidditas*).[33] The linchpin of Aristotelian-Thomistic realism is its claim that this metaphysical essence of an object, which exists materially in external reality in the mode of individuality, is identical to the essence as abstracted and existing immaterially in the concept in the mode of universality. Absent this identity, the universe is hopelessly bifurcated into real and ideal realms.

Although, in the course of chapter 4, we will engage in a lengthy review of the Aristotelian-Thomistic doctrine of "abstraction," let us at this point try to get a better grip on the notion of metaphysical "essence" that undergirds it. According to nominalist and empiricist perspectives, once we can reduce an entity to its more basic constituent elements, we can unmask its "essence" as an archaic and extraneous intellectual encumbrance. The thrust of this form of analysis is to explain the whole in terms of its parts without remainder. Contemporary empirical science, by striving to understand, say, humans, animals, and trees in terms of biochemical processes, arrives at interesting and often fruitful data; however, in this exclusively reductive enterprise, humans, animals, and trees as integral beings are somehow lost. What we are calling critical realism, however, operates in reverse fashion, insisting that the component physical parts of an entity represent *necessary* but not *sufficient* conditions to explain the emergence of a species or natural kind. Such a development must be seen in terms of some higher order of being that accords a specific "form" to more primitive constituent elements. Philosophers such as Aristotle and Aquinas did not claim we had the intuitive capacity to bypass the normal functioning of our senses and to grasp *directly* the metaphysical essences of things. They were led to postulate such essences from their conviction that a materialist analysis (e.g., the ancient Greek atomists') could not adequately account for the structure and intelligibility of the universe we encounter. Hence, they were not obfuscating the discernible contours of reality with their doctrine of metaphysical essences, as was later charged; rather, they were seeking to give a serious, critical, and sufficient account of the universe that our cognitive experience revealed as complex and multi-dimensional.[34]

Maréchal believes that, by helping to revive and refine authentic Aristotelian teaching, Aquinas provided a way for medieval thought to transcend the antinomy of the one and the many, or the apparent contradiction between the deliverance of sense and intellect. Furthermore, he unabashedly contends that

> history also shows that it is not so easy to bring together into one coherent system the totality of the relations which join to being every content of consciousness without exception. From only one point of view may this totality be embraced in its full amplitude. Aristotle, among the Greeks, had the good fortune—or the merit—of discovering it. And St. Thomas, with more assurance and precision, brought medieval philosophy back to this central and dominant position indicated by the Stagyrite.[35]

At first glance, such an exalted claim for a philosophical tradition seems unduly tendentious; it runs directly counter to the pluralist proclivities of our age. Nonetheless, a central tenet of Maréchal's reading of the history of Western thought is that the breakdown of the Aristotelian-Thomistic synthesis in the late Middle Ages, under the impact of nominalism, bequeathed to Renaissance and early modern philosophy a flawed legacy, whose deleterious effects bedevil us to this day.

John Duns Scotus—Philosophical High Wire Act

Although Maréchal pinpoints the full-fledged demise of a unified vision of the deliverance of sense and intellect in the philosophy of William of Ockham, he also claims to see this development prefigured in the work of Scotus. It is a matter of debate among medieval scholars whether Scotus can more accurately be interpreted as a direct precursor of the critical work of Ockham or as a continuator of the constructive, systematic efforts of Aquinas. Without doubt, Scotus is a complex thinker who adroitly weaves together apparently disparate philosophical strands in the creation of his own system.

Scotus was, first and foremost, a Franciscan doctor who was heavily influenced by the Augustinian tradition, and who likewise drew upon the Aristotelian-Thomistic synthesis as well as the thought of the Islamic philosopher Avicenna. But he followed none of his sources slavishly and felt free to criticize major doctrines of previous masters when it seemed warranted. In short, Scotus was an original thinker who deftly employed existing sources in the construction of his own system, and whose fundamental passion was to safeguard the objectivity of human knowledge, especially natural theology.[36]

Maréchal views the work of Scotus as a powerful influence that helped set the stage for the eventual outbreak of nominalism. Certainly Ockham drew inspiration from various thinkers scattered throughout the Middle Ages but, in Maréchal's opinion, the critical bent of his philosophy must be seen as "taking its point of departure from a dogmatic realism of Platonic inspiration in danger of provoking skeptical reactions due to its excessive confidence in the objective value of the concept."[37]

What Maréchal finds objectionable at the heart of Scotus's system is its marked tendency toward creating an isomorphism of concept and reality. To ground the objective nature of conceptual knowledge Scotus maintained that each concept must have an objective referent in the thing under consideration. In this context, Allan B. Wolter, a leading Scotus scholar, writes:

> Scotus . . . argued that if something has the native ability to produce different concepts of itself in the mind, each concept reflecting a partial but incomplete insight into a thing's nature, then the distinction must be in some sense actual. Put in another way, there must be several "formalities" in the thing (where form is understood as the objective basis for a concept and "little form" or formality as an intelligible aspect or feature of a thing that is less than the total intelligible content of a thing).[38]

Scotus holds that we can make a formal distinction between the various "formalities" that make up an object. More precisely, a formal distinction obtains when the mind distinguishes two or more "formalities" or "realities" (*formalitates* or *realitates*) in an object that are physically inseparable but nonetheless conceptually distinct. What is vital for Scotus is that the conceptual distinctions which the mind makes actually exist in reality prior to, and independent of, our own mental operations. In Scotus's own words, "such an entity [i.e. a formality] would be present and in the way that it is present even if no intellect was reflecting upon it, I say that it is present prior to all intellectual operation."[39]

The two most significant formalities that Scotus distinguishes in an object are its "common nature" (*natura communis*) and its "thisness" (*haecceitas*). The common nature is the metaphysical ground of the similarity within a species or natural kind and forms the objective basis for our universal concepts. *Haecceitas* is the final formal determination (*ultima realitas entis*) that makes an object *this* particular object and no other: it functions as the metaphysical principle of individuation in Scotus's system.

As far as his own intention is concerned, Scotus certainly wished to teach a doctrine of critical or moderate realism. His goal was to circumvent the equally distasteful extremes of ultrarealism and nominalism. Like Aquinas, he wanted to demonstrate that our universal concepts are grounded in the particular things we encounter in experience.[40] But Aquinas's ontology is more parsimonious than that of Scotus. Thus, for Aquinas, the dematerialized (hence, deindividualized) *species* abstracted from the phantasm was a sufficient basis for the objectivity of our universal concepts. Scotus, on the other hand, felt it necessary to define the objective ground of our concepts in terms of a specific unity that existed prior to the intellectual operation of abstraction—hence, his doctrine of the "common nature"—defined as "a kind of unity less than numerical unity not dependent on any operation of the intellect."[41]

Maréchal contends that with this doctrine Scotus, however unwittingly, veers dangerously close to ultrarealism. He says of Scotus's epistemology: "As cautious as it might be, this profession of epistemological faith has, without doubt, the appearance of ultrarealism."[42]

Now, ultrarealism is the doctrine that the universal exists in reality as it exists in our minds. It seeks to defend the objectivity of our knowledge by claiming that the logical and the ontological orders are exactly parallel. But, according to Scotus: "If we are speaking in terms of the real order of things, the humanity which is in Socrates, is not the humanity which is in Plato."[43] Furthermore, in line with Aristotle's moderate realism, Scotus explicitly teaches that universals are formed by the intellect; they are not discovered as such in external reality. "The active intellect, concurrent with the common nature, which in itself is indeterminate, is the integral cause of the object in the possible intellect."[44] In Scotus's view, "The common nature in itself is neither universal nor particular, but only a nature."[45] Though potentially singular (particular), it becomes so only through the final formal contraction (*haecceitas*) that confers upon the common nature the status of unique individuality. And though potentially a logical universal, the common nature is only transformed into such by the agency of the active intellect. Moreover, the common nature can never be found existing independently, but only in the mode of singularity in individual things and in the mode of universality in our concepts. Frederick Copleston asserts, "In regard to universals Scotus was certainly not an exaggerated realist. . . . Scotus states unambiguously that the universal in act does not exist except in the intellect."[46]

I agree with Copleston that, strictly speaking, a close textual analysis will not support the claim that Scotus's treatment of universals represents a refined form of ultrarealism. But let us recall a key difference between the respective approaches of Aquinas and Scotus to this issue. Aquinas insists that in the extramental, natural order only individual beings, composed of matter or form, exist. Form is always embodied or materialized and consequently individualized. The process of abstraction mentally isolates form from its embodied (materialized) state as the ontological basis for logical universals. Although, in Aquinas's view, those universals have a foundation in reality (*fundamentum in re*), he never speculates on the status of form as form in some metaphysically indeterminate sense, conceptually prior to individualization in the world or universalization in the mind.

Similarly, Scotus teaches that the common nature can only exist in an individualized state in things (*in re*) and in a universalized state in the mind. Nevertheless, he does hold that we can conceptually isolate it from the aforementioned states and examine its properties by themselves. What then motivates Scotus to do so?

In enunciating his doctrine of the common nature, Scotus was greatly influenced by Avicenna and, hence, the following remarks by Etienne Gilson apply as much to the Subtle Doctor as to the great Islamic thinker:

> Obviously, Avicenna does not mean to say that, taken in themselves, essences actually exist. On the contrary, when he first tells us that essences are to be found either in things or else in minds, what he wants to make clear is that they are not to be found anywhere else. This, at least, is a philosophical statement. But what comes next seems to have little to do with philosophy, and I fancy that this is the explanation. Here is an essence, stone, for instance, which I now find in an intellect and then in particular stones. It is existing according to two different modes. . . . Yet, when I think of it, it is the same essence. . . . If there were no stones, the essence of "stoneness" would still exist, provided only there still be a mind to conceive it, even as a mere possible. On the other hand, if there were stones and no minds to know them, stoneness would still exist in these stones. Consequently, stoneness is in itself wholly unrelated to either minds or things. Hence an almost irresistible psychological illusion to which, in fact, Avicenna falls victim. He has simply imagined as existing in themselves essences which, according to what he himself has just said, never exist in themselves.[47]

When seen through the prism of Gilson's critical analysis, Avicenna's essences and Scotus's common natures appear somewhat like the strange ghosts of Plato's transcendent Ideas. Following Avicenna, Scotus is overzealous in his desire to justify realism and consequently tries to specify what, for human beings, is essentially unspecifiable. We can indeed engage in thought experiments and imagine the essence or nature of "stone" or "horse" in an indeterminate state ontologically prior to individualization in external reality and universalization in the mind, but we must never forget that these imaginings are merely formal constructs having no independent existence of their own, despite our ability to speak as if they do. Gilson's point is that Avicenna and Scotus—their protestations to the contrary notwithstanding—have conjured up for themselves a realm of abstract, eternal, and immutable essences that have ontological priority over the world of becoming in which we actually exist. We simply cannot extract a pure, intelligible world of "being" from the world of "becoming" and still be dealing with *our* world.

So, in the end, Maréchal's accusation of ultrarealism applies to the spirit rather than the letter, to the latent rather than the manifest content of Scotus's philosophy. Maréchal believes that critical realism commits us to discovering intelligibility within our world of becoming, and he is wary of all attempts to construct an intelligible order that seek to circumvent that world.

Maréchal has another criticism of Scotus that we must consider. The Scotist doctrine of the intellectual intuition of the singular (particular) object gives rise to an opposition between the sensible and intellectual orders, thereby leading to what Maréchal calls "the antinomy of sensibility and understanding."[48] In assessing Maréchal's claim, we must once again carefully distinguish between the letter and the spirit (the manifest and latent content) of Scotus's position on this issue.

Scotus does in fact teach that, taken in itself, the individual as individual is intelligible to the intellect. "If the singular is a unified entity, it is intelligible *per se*."[49] Indeed, God and the angels, in Scotus's account, have a direct, intuitive knowledge of the essence of individual objects. But Scotus never claims that, in our current state (*pro statu isto*), we are privy to such an intuitive grasp of things. During our earthly sojourn, in accordance with the ordained power of God (*de potentia Dei ordinata*), the human mind only captures the "existence" of an individual object intuitively. All other knowledge it acquires of that object must come through the active intellect's power of abstracting intelligible forms from the images (phantasms) garnered from sensation. In Scotus's words: "According to ordained power it cannot be said that the singular is intelligible *per se* to any intellect whatsoever, not because the object is not in potency thereto of its own, but because the intellect is only moved by the phantasm, or by the nature that brings forth the phantasm."[50]

In actual practice, then, Scotus envisions the cognitive process proceeding as follows: (1) the senses make contact with extramental reality resulting in the production of the phantasm; (2) in turning toward the phantasm, the intellect becomes intuitively aware of the existence of the external object;

(3) the process of abstraction provides knowledge of the essence of that object. Thus, contrary to Maréchal's claim, the antinomy between sense and intellect does not appear to exist in Scotus's epistemology. In fact, Gilson states that the Scotist distinction between intuitive and abstractive knowledge makes explicit an assumption commonly shared by medieval moderate realists, including Aquinas.

> Duns Scotus here provides a solution to the important problem of the knowledge of existence which essentially accords with that of St. Thomas Aquinas. The two doctrines consider existence as an intuitive intellectual evidence grasped in the sensible. . . . It is from this point of view and for this reason that the Scotist distinction between intuitive cognition and abstractive cognition is of real importance, and it is proper to interpret it as revealing existence, and not using it as an occasion to attribute to Duns Scotus a doctrine as to the intellectual intuition of essence which *pro statu isto* he always refused to grant us.[51]

Having defended Scotus on this score, we must nonetheless add that his system proceeds along a precarious line between Aristotelian realism and Platonic idealism. Unlike Aquinas, Scotus does not accept our cognitive dependence on sense experience as the natural and proper condition of mankind. In his view, the intellect's dependence on the senses is a contingent result of our fallen state. As a superior, immaterial power, the intellect should, strictly speaking, have no necessary recourse to the material powers of the senses to acquire knowledge. In his analysis we can perceive the Platonic (idealist) penchant for demeaning the vagaries of sense-dependent knowledge and the longing for the clear, eternal verities obtained by pure intellectual insight. To be sure, Scotus's dialectical acumen enables him to execute his philosophical high wire act successfully and come out unscathed. Later thinkers, less acute and less firmly anchored in the medieval moderate realist tradition, but sharing these Platonic tendencies, would not be able to duplicate the Subtle Doctor's performance. For them, as we shall see, sense and intellect would become opposing, even irreconcilable, faculties and the dynamic interdependence between them, as enunciated by Aristotle and Aquinas, would gradually be lost.

Thus, Maréchal observes: "Too close to Aristotle to remain simply a disciple of the Seraphic Doctor [St. Bonaventure], but still too little imbued with the peripatetic spirit to unite with Thomism, the Subtle Master [Scotus] occupies an intermediate position whose weakness only his genius could conceal."[52] We have tried to show that the weakness in question consists in an unresolved longing for the clarity and simplicity of Platonic intuitive knowledge at the heart of a system whose external structure is Aristotelian in nature.

William of Ockham—The Eclipse of Medieval Realism

Scotus sought to provide a defense of the objectivity of our knowledge by enunciating what amounted to an isomorphic structure of our concepts with reality. Maréchal explains: "As an impeccable logician, he [Scotus] was led to this formalistic realism, which projects the very modalities of our imperfect and fragmentary intelligence onto the ontological absolute. The reaction against this excess of realism was not long in coming."[53]

The reaction, of course, came in the person of William of Ockham, who employed the Scotist system as a foil against which to propound his own nominalist viewpoint. The approach to philosophy he pursued in the fourteenth century was to have devastating consequences for the metaphysical syntheses of the previous century and, in Maréchal's view, for the subsequent development of Western thought.

Like Scotus, Ockham lists intellectual intuition, sensation, and abstraction as the sources of human knowledge, but he greatly expands the scope and importance of intuition in the cognitive process.[54] In Ockham's view, we have intuitive knowledge not merely of the "existence" of an external object, but of a whole host of basic information about that object that can be immediately apprehended, such as color, size, shape, or location. Ockham also teaches that we can have intuitive knowledge of our own internal states, and that, as Ernest Moody explains, an intuitive cognition is "an act of immediate awareness in virtue of which an evident judgment of contingent fact can be made."[55]

Ockham's position on intuitive knowledge put him in direct conflict with the metaphysical and epistemological assumptions of medieval moderate realism. To thinkers like Aquinas and Scotus, knowledge was first and foremost of the universal or formal element in things. Except for the fact that they exist, individuals could only be known indirectly. This generated concern about the principle of individuation. How can a reality that is primarily known in terms of its metaphysically formal elements manifest itself in the myriad particulars that make up the universe?

Ockham, on the other hand, maintained that the mind could directly intuit many things about existent individuals. As a result, his central question was no longer how to explain individuality but how, in a universe made exclusively of individuals, the mind could form concepts that were universal. In his own words: "We ought not seek some cause of individuation . . . rather we ought to seek how it is possible for anything to be common and universal." [56]

But Maréchal points out that, in Ockham's analysis, it is only the external marks of individuality that the mind attains through intuition.

> The object of individual intuition is not metaphysical individuality, but individual internal or external facts; it is, in a word, concrete experience. And since Ockham does not go so far as to suppose that the contingent diversity of this experience is precontained in the mind, his intuition of the individual . . . belongs to the receptive type. And even, one might say, it is, for the most part, only a transposition of sensible and material experience to the intellect.[57]

Here, Maréchal sees a confusion of the roles of sense and intellect in the cognitive process that would give rise to numerous epistemological conundrums in subsequent centuries. In medieval moderate realism it was only the senses that were receptive. To be sure, the intellect was dependent on the information provided by the senses, but it *actively* isolated the intelligible element latent in the transient flow of sensation to construct an intelligible universe.

With Ockham, on the other hand, knowledge becomes a process of "taking a look out there" for what is to be seen: a move in the direction of the empiricist view of mind as a tabula rasa on which the constant flow of experience makes its imprint. Nonetheless, Ockham does hold for an abstract knowledge of individual things that follows, or is dependent upon, intuitive cognition. For him, abstract knowledge comes in the form of general concepts about individual entities, such as we find in science, that do not concern themselves with any individual in particular.

This leads to the question of the status of universals in Ockham's thought. For one thing, they are not merely words in the sense of conventional or arbitrary signs. The words *man*, *homme*, *homo*, *Mensch*, and *uomo* all give external expression to the concept of a human being which is the same in all possible minds. Ockham sees universals as natural signs produced by the mind which stand for (*supponere*) individuals that sufficiently resemble one another to be grouped together. "Hence we have to say that every universal is one singular thing. Therefore nothing is universal except by signification, by being a sign of several things." [58]

Thus, Ockham is not a nominalist in the strictest sense of the term for he recognizes some kind of *natural* correspondence between similar individuals and the impression they make on our minds. But what is the ground of this similarity? Or, how is it that different individuals cause comparable impressions on our minds? At this point the moderate realist searches for some metaphysical foundation in reality to justify this aspect of our cognitive experience. But Ockham will have none of such speculation. As Philotheus Boehner asserts:

> Ockham refuses to admit that in the real world there is anything that corresponds to the universality of a concept; in other words, he does not admit any universal *in re* common nature, etc.—anything which is not completely individual. . . . Universality, therefore is simply a manner in which a sufficiently generalized abstractive cognition is predictable, and thus it exists wholly within the mind. [59]

Moderate realists will not disagree that universal concepts are individual signs that stand for several particulars, but they do not share Ockham's ontological assertion that reality is exclusively individual in nature. When someone like Aquinas posits a metaphysical foundation in reality (*fundamentum in re*) in his doctrine on universals, he feels compelled to do so if he is to make philosophical sense out of the evident fact that several individuals can be signified by the same sign.

But despite his individualistic ontology, Ockham did not view the universe as constructed of utterly distinct, unrelated entities. As a medieval Christian, he believed that the world had been created by God in accordance with God's ordained power (*potentia Dei ordinata*). Though Ockham spoke of the unfathomable absolute power of God (*potentia Dei absoluta*) vis-à-vis humanity and the universe, he was still confident, through faith, that the countless individual beings that make up the universe find their final meaning and coherence in the fact that they are all products of God's creative agency and under God's constant governance. Hence, for Ockham, the unity of being comes about by an ultimately incomprehensible divine fiat, and not by an intelligible metaphysical order or procession.[60]

It is important to stress the basically theological intent undergirding Ockham's work, lest we anachronistically interpret him as a modern radical empiricist. Ockham believed that the Greek theory of metaphysical essences, introduced into Christian thinking in previous centuries, implied a necessary structure and ordering of the universe that, in his estimation, endangered the central Christian doctrines of divine liberty and omnipotence. He thus set out to purge Christian philosophy of such essences to make room for a purer and undefiled faith. In so doing, Ockham undercut the thirteenth-century ideal—embodied most fully in the work of Aquinas—of the final harmony and compatibility of faith and reason. In its place, we have an uneasy marriage of what amounts to philosophical agnosticism and theological positivism. Ockham was spared the skeptical outcome of his philosophical assumptions by his unquestioned allegiance to Christian beliefs. In generations to come, when these beliefs themselves became problematic, the corrosive consequences of Ockham's critique would be fully manifest.

For one thing, when stripped of both metaphysical and theological foundations, Ockham's complex logic is left hanging in midair. As Maréchal puts it: "Logic ceased having a metaphysical scope. It became a sterile game of symbols that the heirs of Ockham would complicate more and more and empty of content to the point of reducing it to a grammar."[61]

Maréchal's point is that, as a result of Ockham's influence, the rational link between concepts and the individual beings they signify becomes blurred. In the absence of such a link, our conceptual experience, and the languages that are its external expression, hover in an undefined state of limbo in regard to the extramental world. If our logical, universal concepts do not somehow represent reality, then is not the science of logic relegated to a subtle, interesting, but nonetheless subjective enterprise?

According to Maréchal, another consequence of Ockham's critique is the outbreak, once again, of the apparent antinomy of sense and understanding which the Aristotelian-Thomistic synthesis had resolved. In Aquinas's thought, the concept (*verbum mentis*) is a synthetic construction of the understanding (intellect) and the senses. Both understanding and senses remain distinct but are nonetheless united in an intimate, cooperative effort that produces our conceptual knowledge of reality. But, as Maréchal points out:

> With Ockham . . . the synthetic unity of sense and understanding in the direct concept gives way to a simple, extrinsic coordination of sensation and the concept: the senses express in their own way contingent events; the intellect, for its part, perceives them intuitively according to its proper manner. . . . Ockham juxtaposes two faculties within us which seem basically to have the same formal object; we are well assured that sensibility is material, while understanding is immaterial; but, when inspected more closely, the difference is obliterated. Therefore, one of the two faculties becomes superfluous which one should be sacrificed?[62]

Maréchal is asserting that Ockhamist epistemology shattered the primal interdependence of sense and understanding in the cognitive process and instead construed them as two independent sources of knowledge, whose relationship, at best, was problematic. Empiricism would subsequently confront this dilemma by ignoring the constructive role of understanding; conversely, rationalist idealism would belittle the role of sense experience.

According to Maréchal, the second antinomy that Ockham's critique bequeathed to Western thought was between understanding (*ratio, Verstand*) and reason (*intellectus, Vernunft*). In its normal, discursive operations, the human mind, as understanding, aims at a knowledge of things in accordance with their own distinctive essences and functions. Building on this knowledge, the mind, as reason, then strives for a comprehensive vision or rational synthesis of the origin and interrelatedness of all the entities it encounters. In Maréchal's view:

> Ockham's position is very simple: since the rational operation is but an analytical operation on symbols, it lacks all objective validity. In the alternative "understanding or reason," reason, as the understanding's quintessence, as a higher abstraction, cannot claim higher validity than the lower abstractions, which are still near experience and can to some extent be checked. The agnosticism of Ockham is quite logical and derives from his nominalism. One might escape it only by admitting, besides understanding and analytic reason, a *higher reason* which penetrates directly into the mystery of being.[63]

Once, as a result of Ockham's widespread influence, metaphysics is no longer conceived as the "science of being," but merely as an abstract mode of reflecting on particular beings, then our natural intellectual desire to fathom the transcendent, necessary being that grounds the contingent beings of our experience is bereft of philosophical support. Two alternatives remain: either follow the empiricists and claim that whatever transcendent realms there may be—if they exist at all—are in principle unknowable to us; or postulate some higher human faculty, beyond the limitations of sense and understanding, that gives us direct intuitive access to transcendent being or the absolute. According to Maréchal's view, the pursuit of these two alternatives, fueled by the unresolved antinomies that were the legacy of Ockham and his late medieval nominalist successors, is a dominant, underlying influence in the subsequent history of Western philosophy.

A number of scholars now question the Thomists' portrayal of Ockham as a negative force in the history of Western philosophy. They point out that Ockham was not a skeptic as to the mind's capacity to acquire knowledge of the "real" (external)

world. Nor was he encumbered in his epistemological speculations by a sophistic or Academic obsession with absolute certainty or infallibility as criteria for genuine knowledge. As
Marilyn McCord Adams maintains:

> For if, as Ockham joined others in admitting, it is logically possible
> that God should deceive us, the Academic's demand for infallible
> signs by means of which to distinguish genuine from merely appar-
> ent instances of knowledge cannot be satisfied. Rejecting their
> standard, Ockham proceeds to construct a theory according to
> which we can have knowledge that is free from doubt and error and
> that ultimately has its causal origin in sensory intuitive cogni-
> tions.[64]

Hence, if one is looking for a "medieval Hume," one should
consider someone like Nicholas of Autrecourt, rather than
Ockham; for it is Autrecourt who enunciates an explicitly
skeptical posture vis-à-vis the theory of knowledge.[65] Furthermore, recent research into the late medieval period has shown
that the major figures who shaped its intellectual milieu were
a far more diverse lot than formerly suspected.[66]

One must thus be wary of generalized descriptions which
pay insufficient heed to the intricacies and subtle differences
that marked the various thinkers of this era. Ernest Moody
challenges traditional appraisals of Ockhamism, emanating
most notably from the Thomist camp, precisely on this score:

> One may, if he wishes, employ the term "Ockhamism" as a blanket
> designation for all the varied teachings and tendencies of the late
> medieval period, and one may, if he pleases, argue that these later
> doctrines, however opposed to each other or to the teachings of
> Ockham himself, are "logical consequences" of the position of the
> Venerable Inceptor. But such usage is unprofitable, and introduces
> obscurity and confusion into the history of ideas.[67]

Now, it is well to be reminded that responsible scholarship
demands we not facilely project positions onto historical per-
sonages that they, themselves, did not explicitly hold. But it
represents no dereliction of scholarly duty on Maréchal's part
that he attempts to unearth the latent or implicit possibilities
in the work of a past thinker like Ockham which would only

be developed by the subsequent efforts of others. It is likewise well to remember the genuine differences within this group of medieval thinkers. That being said, it is also important to remember that the members of such a group—however much they may disagree on specific issues—can still exhibit a family resemblance in their common allegiance to certain distinctive attitudes or principles. Our desire to do justice to the divergent individual aspects of the speculations of thinkers like Ockham, Adam Wodham, John of Mirecourt, and Nicholas of Autrecourt should not blind us to their shared perspectives as proponents of the *via moderna*: that web of philosophical principles which led them to oppose central aspects of the *via antiqua* of thirteenth-century thinkers like Aquinas and Scotus.[68] Maréchal contends that certain key teachings of Ockham and his loosely defined successors—namely, their anti-realism on the issue of universals, their ontology of discrete particulars contingently linked only by the ordained power of God, and their doctrine of intellectual intuition—set the stage for the epistemological and metaphysical enigmas that would burden the subsequent development of Western thought. In the ensuing chapters, we will attempt to gauge whether Maréchal is correct in this contention. For it is a vital part of his argument in *Le Point de Départ* that we must reappropriate a fundamentally Aristotelian-Thomistic perspective on the nature of knowledge if we are to rehabilitate contemporary philosophical speculation.

CHAPTER TWO

The Plight of
Pre-Kantian Philosophy

Maréchal holds that if metaphysical realism is faithfully to reflect the initial, instinctive thrust of human intelligence toward objective affirmation, it must be grounded in a synthetic theory of the concept in which sense and intellect are conjoined in a primal and irreducible unity of operation.

> That which is *first* given to us, through the natural exercise of our knowledge, is not, as some believed, antinomical terms facing each other in an original hostility and confronting us with the impossible task of reconciling them without changing them. It is rather a synthetic unity, experienced by us in its essential undividedness, and yielding only *afterwards* the relative opposition of its constitutive principles.[1]

What the process of cognition yields in the first instance, then, is not a jumbled juxtaposition of apparently irreconcilable elements, but an integration of these elements into an intelligible *whole*. These elements can, of course, be formally isolated and considered in themselves, but such an undertaking is secondary and derivative: it must not be mistaken for the achievement of a more fundamental viewpoint, epistemologically prior to the original synthesis or integration.

An example will help clarify Maréchal's meaning. Through cognition, we first obtain a concept such as "human being." By reflection, we can attempt to break this concept down into sense data and various other subjective and objective components, but we must not fall prey to the illusion that this reflective operation is more than a second-order enterprise that always presupposes our prior possession of the original and primal concept "human being."

Let us point out a parallel case in biology. Biologists have divided the human being into a variety of basic biological systems, which, in turn, are reduced to more basic biochemical processes. The scientists then study the organism *Homo sapiens* from the viewpoint of these elemental processes. The problem with this approach is that, in seeking to understand the whole in terms of its parts, it distorts the unique status of the whole in question. The human being, as a living, thinking organism, is transformed by the alchemy of reductionist methodology into an assemblage of functionally related biochemical mechanisms.

Maréchal is objecting to a similar reductionist posture in philosophy that fails to do justice to the cognitive priority of the universal concept in the acquisition of knowledge. For him, the particular elements of the cognitive process—the contributions of sense and intellect—can only be understood coherently in relation to the universal concepts they unite to form. When philosophy sheds this central insight, it atomizes our epistemic functions and sets up a false opposition between the intellect and the senses; it only exacerbates the situation when it offers purported solutions to what is essentially a phantom dilemma. For Maréchal, the story of pre-Kantian speculation is an object lesson in how philosophy goes wrong when it misinterprets the primitive and basic synthesis of sense and intellect at the heart of the cognitive process.

Nicholas of Cusa—Mysticism Replaces Metaphysics

The first philosopher Maréchal treats in this context is Nicholas of Cusa. Of him Maréchal asserts: "That which especially attracts our interest in [Nicholas's] philosophy is that it vividly and with a minimum of strange complications shows the reaction of a humanist, an individual and receptive philosopher, to the antinomic elements put into circulation by late scholasticism."[2]

Nicholas of Cusa holds that we human beings have an innate love of truth. This love drives us to seek to know both the finite objects of creation as well as the infinite God, who is their source. The normal discursive functioning of the mind (ratio) searches for truth by means of comparisons and relations between what is certain and what is still in doubt.[3] Hence, we come to know a finite thing by comparing it to what we already know and by taking stock of the myriad similarities and differences that emerge in our comparative analysis. According to Nicholas, however, this incremental process of acquiring knowledge gives us only endless approximations, which may ever more accurately reflect truth, but which never do so in a complete and adequate fashion.[4]

Thus, for Nicholas, our knowledge of finite reality is and always will remain inherently incomplete. Furthermore, he contends that all finite beings mirror the infinite and can only be adequately understood when seen from the infinite or absolute point of view. Based on the neo-Platonic underpinnings of his metaphysical vision, Nicholas asserts that the distinctions and oppositions we perceive in finite entities are identified or synthesized in the infinite, which he accordingly terms the "coincidence of opposites" (coincidentia oppositorum).

Our discursive reason cannot positively apprehend the infinite because: (1) there is no finite object already known that it can properly relate to the infinite; and (2) by the primary rule of discursive reason, the principle of noncontradiction, it cannot grasp the essential nature of the infinite as coincidentia oppositorum. As we augment the fund of relative knowledge that is the province of discursive reason, we should become increasingly aware that philosophy is "learned ignorance" (docta ignorantia): in its normal operation it is utterly ignorant of the absolute source of finite reality.

Nonetheless—once again in accord with his neo-Platonic leanings—Nicholas holds that in addition to discursive reason we possess a superior intuitive form of knowing that he calls intellect (*intellectus*). It can rise above the principle of noncontradiction and apprehend that the final truth of the universe is represented by the *coincidentia oppositorum*: in the infinite all apparent contradiction achieves ultimate unity and harmony. Although, for Nicholas, *intellectus* can intuit the fact that the infinite is the *coincidentia oppositorum*, he does not contend that this higher reason can fathom the infinite's internal movements.[5] What this intuitive insight reveals is that the infinite is beyond human comprehension. Thus, the universe, as the external manifestation of God or the infinite, is likewise ultimately unintelligible to us; we must finally admit that the normal functioning of our rational capacities gives us an essentially distorted picture of reality. For Nicholas, writes Maréchal: "Our abstractive knowledge is not only incomplete, but is definitely false from top to bottom of the scale of the intelligible, because it inevitably locates the ground of finite differences in a rather proximate unity—a genus or a species—when it ought to be referred to God himself."[6]

To better grasp Maréchal's critique, let us compare Nicholas of Cusa's approach to God with Aquinas's. That God is infinitely beyond our finite intellectual capacities is a standard tenet of medieval theology. Aquinas flatly asserts: "The first cause surpasses human understanding and speech. He knows God best who acknowledges that whatever he thinks and says falls short of what God really is."[7] For the medieval tradition, the negative way (*via negativa*) is a means to thwart any idolatrous identification of human conception with the ultimately ineffable reality of God. Put paradoxically, the *via negativa* implies that we approach God more nearly the more fully we comprehend God's infinite difference from all finite reality.[8]

But Aquinas and most of medieval theologians did not, on that account, conclude that reason could say nothing intelligible about God in a positive sense. Indeed, as Aquinas maintains, "unless the human intellect knew something positively about God, it could not deny anything of Him."[9]

In his *Five Ways* (*Quinque Viae*), Aquinas contends that unaided discursive reason can arrive at the conclusion that God exists. In each of the five arguments, he reveals the ontological dependence of finite being on an infinite necessary being that is the efficient, exemplary, and final cause of the universe. It is this ontological dependence of finite creatures on God, the infinite creator and source of all perfections, that forms the objective ground of Aquinas's doctrine of analogy. Thus, he affirms that "whatever is predicated of God and creatures is predicated in virtue of the latter's relation to God as principle and cause in which all the perfections of things pre-exist in a more excellent way." [10]

In enunciating his doctrine of analogy, Aquinas is seeking a critically justified middle position on the truth value of propositions in natural theology. Although he fully accepts and clearly delineates the empirical foundation of all our natural knowledge, including what we may know of God, he finds that the natural and the supernatural, the finite and the infinite, are not irreconcilably opposed: there are traces of the infinite in the finite and of the supernatural in the natural. We must not mistake these traces for a clear and definitive vision, but neither must we allow their partial and incomplete status to reduce us to silence about the existence and nature of God.

Aquinas differs from Nicholas of Cusa in not positing an utterly unbridgeable gap between finite and infinite being. Hence, he sees no need to pose a fundamental antinomy between a lower, discursive reason, inextricably bound to the realm of the finite, and a higher, intuitive reason that can achieve some insight into the absolute or infinite realm. Both thinkers agree that the end (*terminus ad quem*) of all intellectual activity is the mystical contemplation of God. For Aquinas, this mystical end represents the supernatural fulfillment through divine grace of the natural, unlimited desire to know, which is the lifeblood of all cognitive striving. Writing in the spirit of St. Thomas, Maréchal asserts:

The absolute has placed its mark on the fundamental tendency of our intelligence, such that this tendency constantly transcends particular intellections: the mind, through its internal dynamism, is driven from intellection to intellection, from object to object, but as long as it remains in the realm of the finite, it strives in vain to equal its own internal movement. . . . And this unevenness . . . is the very condition of reasoning, the catalyst of that always dissatisfied curiosity in which the scholastics of old rightly discovered the principle of all speculation. Thus, the mind is a faculty in search of its intuition [*une faculté en quête de son intuition*], that is, of assimilation with being, with pure and simple being, supremely one, without restriction, without distinction as to essence and existence or possibility or actuality.[11]

According to this Thomistic view, grace completes nature by elevating the intellect to an intuitive grasp of God that complements the analogical knowledge of God that is possible for us in our embodied state, with its necessary dependence on the empirical data provided by the senses. Thus, our intellectual life, from its most pedestrian to its most lofty operations, is conceived in holistic fashion, with no need to erect artificial oppositions between sense, understanding (*ratio*), and intellect (*intellectus*).

By the time of Nicholas of Cusa, the nominalist drift of Western thought had undercut this holistic intellectual vision and, as a consequence, there set in a despair of philosophy—or, more precisely, of metaphysics—as a satisfactory tool to construct a meaningful universe. In such a milieu, as the great historian of philosophy Etienne Gilson reminds us, people turn to moralism, mysticism, fideism, or some amalgam of these positions, to ward off the corrosive effects of skepticism.[12] Nicholas of Cusa, for his part, chose a neo-Platonic brand of mysticism that attributed the cognitive malaise of his age to the fundamental antinomy between *ratio* and *intellectus* at the heart of fifteenth-century intellectual life. He sought clarity by recourse to the superior intuitive insights of the higher form of reason, *intellectus*. Maréchal describes the cost of such a tactic:

> I would do it without being able to justify my adherence rationally; I would be a fideist or a mystic. And then, by that very fact, I proclaim the inanity of understanding, of analytic reason, all of whose pretensions would be destroyed as soon as one compares them to the absolute, enlightened intelligence. . . . In the end, therefore, in the absence of a supernatural enlightenment, there would only exist in me . . . a single category of objectively true knowledge; direct intellectual and sensible experience.[13]

Maréchal is asserting that, if we follow Nicholas of Cusa's lead and posit an intuitive level of insight distinct and separate from all other intellectual operations, we cut off all possibility of rationally grounding its claims. Furthermore, we radically devalue the accomplishments of discursive reason, and if ever our faith in the intellect as a higher intuitive form of reason should wane, we would be left defenseless against a purely empiricist analysis of knowledge. Thus, in the end, Maréchal pronounces Nicholas's mysticism a failed remedy, no more potent in curing the intellectual ills of Western philosophy than Ockham's fideism.

René Descartes—The Search for Rational Foundations

Maréchal points out that, where Ockham and Cusa sought refuge from philosophical skepticism outside of philosophy, René Descartes strove to combat skepticism by rehabilitating philosophy, by setting it on a sound, indubitable basis. His late medieval and Renaissance predecessors had known little more than scholastic philosophy; when this mode of philosophizing came to apparent rack and ruin as a result of the nominalist critique, they believed that philosophy as such had failed in its quest for truth. But, Gilson tells us, Descartes had a different perspective.

> Descartes brought to the world the unexpected revelation that, even after the breakdown of medieval philosophy, constructive philosophical thinking was still possible. Ever since the fourteenth century there had been men to criticize Aristotle, but Descartes' ambition was quite different: it was to replace him.[14]

According to Maréchal, Descartes's work captured the imagination of his epoch because it responded to the three basic demands of human thought: "(1) the eternal demand for a metaphysics; (2) the demand for rational unity in speculation; and (3) the demand for a harmony of philosophical doctrines with the theoretical and practical interests of the time."[15]

Hence, for Maréchal, the metaphysical impulse is an ultimately ineradicable aspect of our being in the world. The ongoing desire for answers to metaphysical questions concerning God, human beings, and the ultimate nature of the universe cannot be utterly extinguished. During deconstructive periods, this desire may be forced to seek nonphilosophical outlets, or to go underground and lie dormant as a vague longing, until a constructive thinker again dares to expound a new metaphysical vision that offers hope for fulfillment.

For Descartes, it was mathematics, with its clear and definitive demonstrations, that was to serve as a model for the reconstruction of philosophy.[16] Descartes envisioned a "universal mathematics," a unified scientific and philosophical framework in which each element possessed the clarity, distinctness, and certainty of demonstrations in arithmetic and geometry. And he saw in the *cogito* and the knowledge of God and extended matter (*res extensa*) simple, evident notions equal in cognitive force to the concepts found in arithmetic and geometry.

Philosophy, according to Descartes, must be restructured on clear and distinct ideas, and not muddled with mere opinions or probabilities, even if they have the weight of authority and tradition. Such clear and distinct ideas are the product of intellectual intuition, a faculty he describes as follows:

> By "intuition" I do not mean the fluctuating testimony of the senses or the deceptive judgement of the imagination as it botches things together, but the conception of a clear and attentive mind, which is so easy and distinct that there can be no room for doubt about what we are understanding. Alternatively, and this comes to the same thing, intuition is the indubitable conception of a clear and attentive mind which proceeds solely from the light of reason.[17]

Descartes believed he had discovered a method for attaining a level of truth that was free from doubt or error, free from the uncertainty of sensation, the vagaries of the imagination, and the disputes of so-called authorities. The clear, penetrating light of intellectual intuition, already present in the insights and workings of mathematical reasoning, should be extended to our scrutiny of the totality of reality.

To set philosophy on an indubitable foundation, Descartes needed an unassailable starting point that could not be undercut by skeptical doubt. He therefore went on the offensive, using "methodic doubt" to clear the mind of obscurities, uncertainties, and probabilities so that it could arrive at truth in its purity and simplicity.

Descartes enunciates his famed *cogito ergo sum* as the sure foundation of his philosophical system. The Cartesian *cogito* is the equivalent of conscious awareness as such.[18] I do not argue to the fact that "I exist" (*sum*), but I perceive directly, in one simple and evident intuition, that doubting, thinking, and existing are inseparable.

But what is the status of the "self" (*ego*) in Descartes's system? Maréchal asserts that "in [Descartes'] view, existence that is clearly (necessarily) thought and real existence in the metaphysical sense correspond with one another in virtue of the parallelism he postulates between our 'clear and distinct' concepts and things."[19] Hence, for Descartes, if we can clearly and distinctly intuit the self as an independent, coherent thinking substance (*res cogitans*), this establishes its real existence; and, from this purportedly sure and certain knowledge of the self, Descartes then systematically proceeds to deduce an entire metaphysics.

But does Descartes's *cogito ergo sum* enjoy the kind of indubitable certitude that he imagines? Maréchal responds: "This indubitability belongs to the phenomenon: I can always, at least provisionally, doubt the ontological significance of an appearance, but not an appearance as appearance. The '*cogito ergo sum*' is incontestably true in the phenomenal order. But what can we deduce from that?"[20]

In other words, Descartes provides us with only a subjective or psychological certitude. He temporarily suspends the uncertainties of sense knowledge—our immediate means of contact with external reality—to achieve a supposedly indubitable epistemic point of departure. Having done so, he can then confidently proclaim that our concepts are not just mental fictions only by assuming an identity of thought and being that is ultimately grounded in the belief that God would not deceive us.[21]

In Descartes's philosophy, the senses and the understanding (intellect) are externally but not internally related; and this external relation amounts to a theological tour de force that leaves the apparent antinomy between sense and understanding philosophically unresolved. Descartes reasons that God, as the perfect being, could not have created a world in which our "clear and distinct ideas" did not correspond to external reality. Where Ockham turned to fideism to escape the skepticism implicit in his nominalist empiricism, Descartes turns to faith in the veracity of God to escape the subjectivism implicit in his idealism. In the final analysis, it is this faith, and not the rationally convincing nature of philosophical argumentation, that guarantees the reliability of Descartes's "clear and distinct ideas." We can see here the ontologistic roots of Descartes's thought that Malebranche would later make explicit.

When viewed in its totality, the Cartesian corpus offers us a metaphysics that is pure spiritualism and a physics that is pure mechanism. The antinomy of sense and understanding that first broke out in late medieval philosophy has, in Descartes, developed into an ontological rift that divides reality into two essentially incompatible spheres. This rift generated a series of philosophical conundrums that would plague Descartes and his successors for generations; to give an outstanding example: Does there exist an external world that is the objective referent of our "clear and distinct ideas"?

Cartesian epistemology makes it impossible to conceive of any but an artificial relationship between sense and understanding in the cognitive process. As dispensable as sense knowledge appears to be in Descartes's framework, he does not go on to expound a thoroughgoing idealism, but struggles instead to find some role for sensation in his account of knowledge. Although he finds no need of sense experience to explain the innate ideas of self, God, or mathematical and logical axioms, Descartes does maintain that our other ideas are somehow images or copies of the external world, in which sense perception plays some part. But his metaphysical dualism, which divides reality into *res cogitans* and *res extensa*, leaves Descartes in the throes of an inescapable dilemma: How can the senses—connected as they are with a material (extended) body—possibly interact with an immaterial (spaceless or unextended) mind? Descartes' sorry speculations about the pineal gland have the air of philosophical desperation that usually arises when a thinker has created a problem that is insoluble according to his own principles.

Maréchal summarizes his appraisal of Descartes' epistemological efforts in the following terms: "Despite the originality of the effort from which it derived, Cartesian epistemology has contributed no really new constructive principles. Descartes deserves credit for having tried to find for philosophy a starting point which might be wholly certain, but he has not instituted the integral critique of the *presupposita* [presuppositions] of knowledge."[22]

Thus, in Maréchal's view, even though Descartes offered no satisfactory solution to the antinomies that were the legacy of late medieval thought, he did provide us with a rationalistic dogmatism: a doctrine that our intellect or understanding can establish and explicate an objective metaphysical order that is only minimally related to the unreliable data provided by our senses.

Unfortunately, neither Descartes nor his Cartesian successors could successfully relate this ideal, metaphysical order to the empirical realm that lay outside the mind without invoking some contrived linkage that, in the end, could not stand the test of critical scrutiny. As this failure became more evident, the time became ripe for an empiricist reaction against a rationalist idealism that seemed so divorced from actual sense experience.

Thus, we can draw a parallel between the Ockhamist reaction to Scotus's philosophy and the empiricist reaction to Cartesian rationalism. Both seek to vindicate the empirical element in our knowledge against an idealist emphasis that devalues its significance. In reaffirming the empirical basis of our knowledge, both show themselves to be heirs, at least in part, to the Aristotelian tradition. But both, largely due to their nominalist presuppositions, fail to appropriate the totality of the Aristotelian patrimony. They correctly highlight the empirical side of Aristotle's thought, but overlook the "critical realist" matrix in which it is set; that is, they fail to appreciate the centrality of Aristotle's doctrine of universals to his epistemological and metaphysical endeavors. Once removed from this matrix, Aristotle's empiricism is seriously deformed. The result is an agnostic or skeptical attitude toward any underlying metaphysical dimension that can account for the order of the universe revealed through the senses. Ockham was spared this outcome by his theological assertion of an overarching universal order established by the ordained power of God. But, by

Hume's time, such a fideist intrusion into philosophical analysis would lose most of its plausibility, and, as a result, the skeptical import of empiricism could no longer be forestalled.

Before considering this empiricist turn in Western thought, let us complete our overview of Maréchal's analysis of Cartesian rationalism by turning to the most prominent thinkers who sought to perfect what Descartes had begun.

Nicolas Malebranche—The Vision of All Things in God

Descartes' major successors, Malebranche, Spinoza, and Leibniz, saw that he had failed to give an adequate account of the relation between the mind and the senses. Nonetheless, in their attempts to overcome his failure, they all remained firmly within the purview of Descartes' fundamental assumptions.[23]

Each of these three thinkers accepted the validity of Descartes' demonstration that mind and matter are two completely distinct realities, but it also seemed evident to them that mind and matter (intellect and senses) are somehow related. Thus, in their analysis, absolute idealism did not appear a viable solution to the Cartesian dilemma. The only alternative, then, was to appeal to God—whose existence Descartes had clearly established—as the binding force that joined the otherwise disparate substances of mind and matter in the cognitive process.

In this context Malebranche frankly asserts: "To know God's works, we must attend, not to the sensations which we have of them, but to the ideas which represent them. For I cannot reiterate too often that we must consult not the senses and their respective modalities, which are sheer darkness, but Reason which enlightens us by its divine ideas, by ideas that are immutable, necessary, eternal."[24]

In Malebranche's view, the information provided by our senses is vitiated because it is subject to error; our only reliable source of knowledge stems from our "clear and distinct ideas," which are, in fact, the ideas or archetypes of objects in the mind of God.

Maréchal comments on Malebranche's "vision in God" (*vision en Dieu*) as follows: "The history and the internal connection of doctrines equally show that this dogmatic intuitionism is one of the logical outcomes of Cartesianism. While the

Cartesian epistemology remains wavering, that of Malebranche goes right to the end of the dogmatic line in which it is tending; it completes it."[25]

Descartes, himself, considered the possibility that a *vision en Dieu* was the source of our ideas about the external world, but he rejected this thesis:

> For God has given me no faculty at all for recognizing any such source for these ideas; on the contrary, he has given me a great propensity to believe that they are produced by corporeal things. So I do not see how God could be understood to be anything but a deceiver if the ideas were transmitted from a source other than corporeal things. It follows that corporeal things exist.[26]

Because, as we have seen, the reliability of those ideas ultimately rested on the assumption that God, who has endowed us with this inclination, was not a deceiver, Descartes's mind-body dualism made an integral relation between these external, corporeal objects and our internal, nonmaterial ideas impossible. Realizing this, Malebranche strove to give an account of our conceptualizations of external reality in terms of a mental capacity to intuit the divine ideas directly.

Was there then any need at all to posit an essential role for sensation in the cognitive process? Logically, one might have expected Malebranche to respond negatively, and to proceed to elucidate a brand of idealism akin to what Berkeley would later propound. But theologically, due to his belief in the creation of the material universe by God, Malebranche could not accept such a radical turn. Instead, he took recourse in the doctrine of "occasionalism": at each occasion that we take for mind-body interaction, it is actually the divine agency which brings about the necessary changes in both realms in parallel fashion. Malebranche thereby hoped to salvage some place for sensation in the cognitive process that did not violate the integrity of the Cartesian mind-body dualism.

To grasp the underlying logic of this doctrine, it is important to note that, strictly speaking, occasionalism is not confined to the mind-body problem, but enunciates a general view of all bodies in the universe. Malebranche contends that the idea of extension does not itself imply mobility. Consequently, he considers the ancient and medieval view that bodies have some internal power or faculty, which accords them the capacity for self-movement or the ability to move others, as an unwarranted projection of human, spiritual capacities onto inert matter. He is thus led to expound a totally theocentric vision of the universe, in which God is not only creator and preserver, but also directly involved in all movement or change.[27]

Now, if bodies cannot move other bodies, then a fortiori they cannot move minds; and, given the presupposition of Cartesian dualism, the reverse is likewise impossible. So, in regard to cognition, Malebranche concludes that, on the occasion of certain physical states in the body, God (in accordance with his own freely established laws) induces corresponding states in the mind. This, he holds, is a properly philosophical way to account for the apparent coordination of mind and body in cognition.

Maréchal points out that, despite Malebranche's fulminations against the pantheism of Spinoza, there is a real affinity between Malebranche's doctrine of occasionalism and Spinoza's monism of substance. The Cartesian ontology allowed for three fundamental realities in the universe: God, mind, and extended matter. In Malebranche's system, the latter two are fundamentally passive pawns of God's complete and universal causal efficacy. Once we deny to mind and matter any capacity for efficient causality, once God becomes the unique cause of all events, what genuine metaphysical role do mind and matter play, except perhaps as attributes of the one, all-encompassing substance, God? As Maréchal notes: "Despite himself, Malebranche was engaged in a course which leads to Spinozism."[28]

But in Malebranche's thought we can also see the possibility of the consistently idealist turn in philosophy that Berkeley would execute later in the eighteenth century. If God is the exclusive causal agent in the universe, and if our minds are never in direct contact with an external world, what metaphysical guarantee do we have of that world's existence? Furthermore, what need do we have to posit its existence in the first place? In the light of Malebranche's theocentric epistemology, it would appear more parsimonious to account for our cognitive experience exclusively in terms of our minds and God.

How does Malebranche attempt to elude the conclusion that a rigorous application of his principles leads more naturally to metaphysical monism or idealism than to the dualism he was trying to defend? He simply proclaims: "I am assured that bodies exist, not just by the natural revelation of sensations which God gives me of them, but far more still by the supernatural revelation of faith."[29] For Malebranche, it is the revelation contained in scripture that God alone created the material world which serves as the ultimate guarantee of its independent existence. Ironically, then, Malebranche, who set out to salvage Cartesian dualism by adequately depicting the relation between mental and material reality in Cartesian terms, unwittingly demonstrates that, without a fideist appeal to scripture, this dualism must dissolve itself into monism or idealism.

Benedict Spinoza—Integral Rationalism

Although it would be misleading to portray Spinoza as a mere successor to Descartes—other influences, notably the Jewish mystical tradition, were operative in his thought—he nonetheless functioned within a fundamentally Cartesian framework. Spinoza accepted the Cartesian parallelism between ideas and reality, as well as the claim that true knowledge was to be achieved in the form of "clear and distinct ideas." But, as Maréchal affirms:

> The criterion of clear ideas in Spinoza presents a more comprehensive fullness and sets up rationalist claims more frankly radical than in Descartes. The clarity of an idea is not to be separated . . . from the entire coherence of the system in which it is contained. This demand for total rationality is legitimate, for it represents a profound condition for the natural functioning of our minds.[30]

Spinoza thus expounds an integral rationalism in which the truth of any proposition is based on its relation to a total system of interlocking and interdependent propositions. This system, in turn, reflects the interrelated nature of reality as such. To achieve the holistic, rational vision at which Spinoza aims, we must move beyond a limited, empirical-temporal viewpoint, which considers individual beings in isolation, and rise to a panoramic intellectual vista, from which individual entities are contemplated in relation to the all-encompassing, infinite, and perfect being of which they are a part.[31] It is a major goal of

Spinoza's philosophical endeavors to correct our common intellectual outlook (*emendatio intellectus*), so that we, too, might ascend to this superior way of envisaging the universal order.

Although Spinoza shares the fundamental Cartesian assumption as to the parallelism that exists between the ideal and real orders of being, he develops its implications in a way that other followers of Descartes and, of course, Descartes himself would roundly reject. With this parallelism as his basis, Spinoza treats all relations in the universe (even those of physical causality) as if they were necessary relations of logical (mathematical) implication. In his view, a bona fide causal explanation must *necessarily* account for the existence of a substance and distinguish it from all else. In Spinoza's own words: "By an adequate cause, I mean a cause through which its effect can be clearly and distinctly perceived. By an inadequate or partial cause, I mean a cause through which, by itself, its effect cannot be understood."[32]

As a result, only God, the infinite and necessary being, can be considered a true causal agent: any other conceivable causal force in the universe will involve some degree of partialness and contingency and thereby provide an inadequate explanation of the logical-mathematical necessity that governs the workings of the cosmos. We saw that Malebranche attributed complete causal efficacy to God but stopped short of constructing a monistic metaphysics because of his religious scruples. Unfettered by such scruples, Spinoza pursued what he believed to be the inexorable logic of the rationalist approach to reality to its inescapable conclusion.

In part, Spinoza faithfully echoed the Cartesian idea of "substance" as that which exists independently. Strictly speaking, only God, who alone is *causa sui*, merits the designation of "substance." Nevertheless, Descartes felt justified in applying the term to those finite realities which enjoyed a relative degree of existential independence, that is, which "need only the concurrence of God in order to exist."[33] However inconsistent within the logic of his system, Descartes's attribution of "substance" to those entities that possessed only relatively independent existence enabled him to construct a philosophical dualism that exhibited at least a prima facie consistency with traditional Christian theism.

On the other hand, as Maréchal observes: "Spinoza, free from doctrinal scruples, and more unrelentingly faithful to his epistemological point of departure, dropped as irrelevant the concessions Descartes made to a scholasticism that accorded little with the absolute realism of the concepts of our understanding."[34] Spinoza draws the conclusion that God alone, as *causa sui*, enjoys absolutely independent existence, and is thus the sole and unique substance.[35] Finite realities must be seen as mere attributes of God.[36]

Spinoza's monistic ontology leads him simply to dissolve the mind-body dualism, which had ensnared Cartesian thought, in favor of what we might call a psycho-physical parallelism. Mind and body are not distinctly different realities which cannot interact; rather they constitute two attributes or manifestations of the one underlying, infinite reality. Since they are both aspects of the same, unique metaphysical substance, whatever affects mind affects body, and vice versa.

Finally, for Spinoza, "nothing in the universe is contingent, but all things are conditioned to exist and operate in a particular manner by the necessity of the divine nature."[37] Once true causality is defined in terms of necessary logical relations, and God is seen as the sole causal agent, then all contingency in the universe can only be apparent, resulting from a partial or inadequate understanding of the ultimate nature of things.

Cartesian rationalism was inspired by the desire for a comprehensive system that could explicate reality with unassailable certitude. Because an epistemology based on our relation to the external world via the senses could not fulfill this desire, Descartes turned to intellectual intuition and the realm of "clear and distinct ideas" for his epistemic starting point. But having initially isolated himself from the sensual or physical realm, Descartes sought an assurance that our ideas do, in some way, correspond to the reality of the extended material universe. In need of a bridge between the ideal and the physical realms, Descartes took refuge in God as his metaphysical bridge builder.

Spinoza countered by arguing that the ideal and physical orders are in fact one, and only appear as disparate when viewed in an inadequate fashion. Viewed from the highest intellectual perspective, sub specie aeternitatis, the apparent divisions and contingencies of the universe are subsumed in one unified and necessary whole. It is only from this lofty perch that the original goal of Cartesian certainty can be attained.

Maréchal considers Spinoza's work a marvelously consistent example of what he calls a metaphysics of the understanding: "Such a metaphysics is based entirely on the analytic relations of our objective concepts, accepted as such, ready made, as a direct representation of ontological reality without any other critique of their validity than the mere logical coherence of the deductive connection by which they derive one from another."[38]

This uncritical realism of the understanding fosters the assumption that the ideal and real orders are exactly parallel. On this basis, Spinoza can elaborate a purely deductive metaphysics in which causality is reduced to exclusively analytic-logical connections, which leads, in turn, to a radical devaluation of sense knowledge. Maréchal explains: "Contingency, which is absent from things and absent from 'adequate ideas' or true intelligibles, does not slip into our knowledge except by means of 'inadequate ideas,' ideas which are confused because they are incompletely grasped and which are deformed from the mind's perspective by their proximity to the body."[39]

As we have mentioned, the goal of Spinoza's philosophical endeavors is to effect an intellectual transformation whereby we transcend the inadequate perspective of sense knowledge for an eternal vision of the one absolute substance and its attributes or modifications, governed totally by an inexorable logical necessity. In Maréchal's view, such a move does not eliminate the antinomy between sense and understanding, or between what is necessary and what is contingent in our knowledge.

> Here, once again, the contingent element in our knowledge is reduced to a subjective, imperfect and provisional appearance. To pass from the contingent to the necessary is not to change an object or to acquire something or other; it is only to pass from one attitude to another, to effect an interior restoration.[40]

The certainty and serenity of Spinoza's metaphysics rest on a thoroughgoing rationalist determinism which can in no way take seriously the contributions of sense experience in the acquisition of knowledge. Such a system cannot resolve the antinomy between sense and understanding in some sort of dynamic synthesis, but simply relegates the component of sensation to what is, in effect, a subjective or illusory status.

Furthermore, Maréchal points out, Spinoza's monism is based on his assumption about the absolute realism of our conceptual grasp of being, and represents "the transposition into the absolute of the concretive mode of our concepts."[41] This uncritical realism leads Spinoza to assert that absolute reality must have the same structure as our objective concepts, understood in the Cartesian sense of "clear and distinct ideas." In such an outlook, a transcendent God—one who cannot be adequately represented by our conceptual scheme—is literally unthinkable because the range of concept and reality are assumed to be coextensive. Hence, traditional theism must be ruled out and replaced by monism or pantheism.

This absolute realism lay at the heart of Cartesian rationalism and was of course shared by Descartes and Malebranche. But because these French thinkers were wedded to a theological tradition which insisted that God was a transcendent reality, they remained—albeit inconsistently—both theists and dualists. Unencumbered by that tradition, Spinoza felt free to work out the monistic-pantheistic worldview implicit in the epistemological starting point of Cartesian rationalism.

Such a worldview obliterated the Thomistic distinction between "signification" and "representation" in relation to our conceptual abilities. This distinction rested partly on a frank admission of the empirical basis of all human conceptualizing, and partly on the innate, human intellectual dynamism or unlimited desire to know. It meant that not everything we intended by our concepts (signification) could be pictured (representation) before something like the mind's eye. We had no direct access to reality that could simply dispense with the medium of sense experience. But it also meant that the intellect, as the dynamic, self-transcending capacity that sought an intelligible order underlying manifold sense experience, could point in the direction of levels of reality that were not subject to direct conceptual representation because they transcended the domain of the senses. Such reasoning led Thomists to assert that the concept of a transcendent God, that is, one who

could be signified but not adequately represented by our conceptual scheme, was not meaningless, empty, or unthinkable. As a Thomist and a critical realist, Maréchal, of course, affirms a certain correspondence between thought and being. But he does so on the basis of a fundamental complementarity of sense experience and human intellectual dynamism as interdependent modes for apprehending being, and not on the Cartesian grounds of a superior form of intellectual insight that purportedly rectifies the inadequacies of sensation.[42] Thus, Maréchal rejects the Cartesian intuitive approach to reality and its quest for a deductively certain metaphysical system. In the Aristotelian-Thomistic spirit, he wishes to construct an inductive, empirically based metaphysics.

If Maréchal's Transcendental Thomism is to be adjudged a viable option in the current philosophical scene, it must rise above static, ahistorical approaches to knowledge in favor of a dynamic posture that enables us somehow to chart a course between an uncritical foundationalism, on the one hand, and an unlivable relativism, on the other. In short, what is required today in the way of epistemology and metaphysics is a rational support and justification for our dedication to truth, not as a once-and-for-all possession, but as an ever-expanding achievement to be passionately pursued. Crucial to a proper appraisal of the current import of Maréchal's work will be a precise explication and critique of his understanding of the internal dynamism of the intellect insofar as it motivates and directs such a pursuit.

Gottfried Leibniz—The Attempt at Synthesis

The final Cartesian rationalist considered by Maréchal, Gottfried Leibniz, took a more conciliatory approach to the philosophy of his ancient and medieval predecessors. According to Maréchal: "Knowing at once the Scholastics and the Cartesians, [Leibniz] strove to borrow from each what was best in order to compose his own system, instead of opting for one of the two doctrines in partisan fashion."[43]

More specifically, Leibniz saw the need to complement Cartesian mechanism with Aristotelian dynamism. The mechanistic view, on its own, was insufficient to account for the dynamic nature of reality. However accurately it described movement (change) in the universe, in the sense that movement tended to occur according to regular and predictable laws or patterns, it did not explain the source and end of movement (change) as such. Leibniz fully realized that unenlightened Aristotelians had in the past misused the metaphysical notions of "formal" and "final" causality, to the neglect of a scientific analysis of the "efficient" causality operative in the physical dimension of the universe. It was against the background of such misuse that he understood the passion of his age to banish "form" and "purpose" (*telos*) from the philosophical lexicon. But, in Leibniz's view, the reactive suppression of these traditional metaphysical notions had outlived its usefulness, and he therefore strove to reintroduce them into an overall analysis of the structure and functioning of reality.[44]

Thus, on the cosmic scale, Leibniz stresses the teleological dimension of the universe. It is true that nature, in its physical forms, is impelled and controlled mechanically by specific efficient causes, but this process serves as an effective means to achieve God's ends or purposes in accordance with the principle of "fitness."[45]

Leibniz not only wanted to make room for a dynamic concept of substance within the Cartesian framework, he also sought to defend the pluralism of substance against Spinoza's monism. Leibniz held that the fundamental experience of individual self-consciousness as a distinct, self-contained unity in the Cartesian *cogito* ruled out the possibility of his taking a monistic metaphysics seriously.

Leibniz teaches that the universe is composed of an infinite number of simple substances called monads, which are "the true atoms of nature, and, in a word, the elements of things."[46] These monads are active and undergo change, but it is in accordance with their own internal dynamism (*telos*), not on account of some external pressure caused by interaction. Hence, "monads have no windows, by which anything could come in or go out."[47] All monads have rudimentary perceptions—the internal condition of the monad representing external things—but only those monads which enjoy the power of apperception (consciousness or reflective knowledge) are rational souls. It is this latter power which "makes us capable of understanding science or demonstrative knowledge."[48]

Although Leibniz defines a living substance as a monad with its particular body, nowhere does he give a clear account of the emergence of matter from the nonmaterial monads which are the metaphysical building blocks of the universe. His obscurity on this central issue leaves the external world, at best, tottering in a state of metaphysical limbo; at worst, matter is mere phenomenal appearance that philosophical analysis can dissolve into its proper nonmaterial or spiritual components.

Since, in Leibniz, "our representation of extension, far from being a 'clear and distinct idea,' would only be the confused state of an idea of order,"[49] Maréchal concludes that, despite this thinker's intentions, he does not succeed in overcoming the Cartesian inability to relate the physical and spiritual levels of being coherently. In Leibniz's system, matter is treated as a confused perception, since the ultimate constituents or reality are the isolated spiritual monads. Notwithstanding his assertion of pluralism against the monism of Spinoza, Leibniz nonetheless denies any metaphysical independence to the material level of being. Furthermore, his employment of the doctrine of "pre-established harmony" to explain the correspondence between otherwise noninteracting monads, while not as crude as Malebranche's occasionalism, is nevertheless a gratuitous appeal to divine intervention to resolve a metaphysical dilemma.

According to Maréchal, Leibniz is, in the end, no more successful than his predecessors in constructing a coherent metaphysical vision on Cartesian principles. Maréchal traces the failure of the Cartesian rationalists to their uncritical acceptance of the late medieval doctrine of *species specialissima*, that is, the intuitive grasp of concrete singulars by the intellect. This application of the role of material sensibility to the intellect resulted in a steady devaluation of the function of the senses in acquiring knowledge. Among the Cartesians the senses are, at best, a mere extrinsic occasion for the intellect's operations. As a result, the complementary roles of sense and intellect in the cognitive process are obscured, along with the synthetic nature of the concepts that this process produces. Once the vital interdependence of sense and intellect is blurred, then the human person is no longer seen as a substantial unity of body and soul, but as a duality of body (*res extensa*) and mind (*res cogitans*). The history of Cartesian rationalism indicates that, after the bifurcation effected by Descartes's analysis, the human person became like a philosophical Humpty-Dumpty after the fabled fall, and neither Descartes nor his successors could coherently reconstruct the shattered creature as long as they stayed within the ambit of Cartesian assumptions.

John Locke—Empiricism at the Halfway Point

At the forefront of another grand pre-Kantian philosophical movement examined by Maréchal, empiricist John Locke tried to counter the excesses of continental rationalism, especially the doctrine of innate ideas, by returning to Aristotle's emphasis on the sense-dependent nature of our knowledge. Of course, Aquinas had employed this same empirical emphasis as the cornerstone of his philosophizing but with results far different from those of Locke and his empiricist offspring.

The first philosopher to devote his main efforts to an exploration of epistemology, Locke sets as the purpose of his major work, *Essay Concerning Human Understanding*, "to enquire into the original [*sic*], certainty, and extent of human knowledge."[50] He begins by vaguely defining "idea" as "whatever is the object of understanding when man thinks."[51] He argues that there are no innate ideas, for they all stem from experience, that is, sensation and reflection. Sensation is the source of experience. External objects impinge upon the mind via the senses, and give rise to ideas such as "yellow, white, heat, cold, soft, hard, bitter, sweet and all those which we call sensible qualities."[52] Reflection provides us with the second source of ideas as it attends to internal, mental operations such as "perception, thinking, doubting, believing, reasoning, knowing, willing."[53]

Locke goes on to distinguish simple from complex ideas. The former are received passively by the mind, while the mind plays an active role in the formation of the latter. By combining simple ideas such as "whiteness," "sweetness," and "hardness," the mind can form the complex idea of "sugar." In addition, by "bringing two ideas, whether simple or complex, together and setting them by one another, so as to take a view of them at once without uniting them into one,"[54] the mind gets its ideas of relations. Finally, the mind can form general ideas (nominal universals) by abstracting them "from all other ideas that accompany them in their real existence."[55]

The question arises: How does Locke relate our myriad, multifaceted ideas to the external world? In this context, he makes a distinction between "ideas" and "qualities": "Whatsoever the mind perceives in itself, or is the immediate object of perception, thought, or understanding that I call idea; and the power to produce an idea in our mind, I call quality of the subject wherein that power is."[56]

Thus, Locke assumes a causal relationship between external objects and the mind: an object, such as a snowball, has certain powers or qualities to produce in us certain ideas such as "white," "cold," and "round." But Locke divides these qualities into the categories of "primary" and "secondary." "Primary qualities" (solidity, extension, figure, mobility) are inseparable from a body, and the ideas they give rise to are resemblances of bodies. Therefore, Locke affirms that "their patterns do really exist in the bodies themselves."[57] But "secondary qualities," such as color, sound, taste, and odor, are "nothing in the objects themselves but powers to produce various sensations in us by their primary qualities."[58] In sum, Locke maintains that our idea of the shape of, say, a rose really corresponds to the figure embodied in the flower itself; but our idea of its color is only the result of the interaction of the primary qualities of the rose and our visual capacities. The "redness" of the rose cannot be said to be contained in the flower itself.

From a Thomist perspective, Locke's reasoning is muddled by his failure to clarify whether ideas are indeed the objects of knowledge (*id quod intelligitur*) or the means by which we come to know external reality (*id quo intelligitur*).[59] In describing the relationship between the mind and external objects, Locke uncritically employs a realist "correspondence language" that his declared epistemological starting point— namely, ideas are the object of knowledge—will not allow. Locke, however, does seek a practical egress from this dilemma by a series of commonsense arguments like the following: "I ask anyone, whether he be not invincibly conscious to himself of a different perception when he looks on the sun by day, and thinks of it by night; when he actually tastes wormwood, or smells a rose, or only thinks on that savour or odour."[60] Locke, then, simply assumes that common sense warrants the assumption that sensations have causes outside the mind and that these external stimuli resemble the sensations to which they give rise.[61] But if, in accordance with Locke's stated epistemological principles, we only experience the sensations—or what Locke loosely calls "ideas"—and not their causes, what philosophical warrant do we have to assume the existence of such causes?

Maréchal responds to Locke's use of common sense by asserting: "In truth, Locke is an unconscious dogmatist, an empiricist who remains at the half-way point."[62] Unwilling to push his empiricist principles to their logical outcome, namely, metaphysical skepticism, Locke uncritically appeals to common sense as a way to salvage some semblance of philosophical realism.

Furthermore, as Maréchal points out, what Locke provides is a psychological, rather than a truly metaphysical, analysis of knowledge. If one begins by considering ideas as the primary object of knowledge, one is thereby imprisoned in a philosophical subjectivity from which there is no rational escape. Against such a subjective, one-sided investigation of knowledge, Maréchal claims that

> every system which reaches a metaphysics of knowledge must emphasize the consideration of the subject. For the relation of knowledge necessarily enters into an ontological system as an immanent synthesis of subject and object. . . . The subject can define the value of the object only in so far as, *identified with the object* [emphasis added], it remains opposed to it.[63]

In line with his Aristotelian-Thomistic roots, Maréchal is here arguing for an epistemological starting point that views ideas as the *means* by which we come into immediate contact with the external world. On this account, the senses, the intellect, and the world are joined in a primal relationship from which knowledge emerges. One of the key insights that one garners from Maréchal's reading of the history of Western philosophy is that any approach to knowledge that severs this fundamental epistemic triad, and discounts or suppresses one or more of its members, is destined from the outset to provide a partial and distorted analysis of how we come to know.

George Berkeley and David Hume—The Return of Skepticism

Of Locke, Bertrand Russell once wrote: "No one has yet succeeded in inventing a philosophy at once credible and self-consistent. Locke aimed at credibility, and achieved it at the expense of consistency."[64] Unlike Lord Russell, George Berkeley and David Hume found Locke, in part, incredible precisely because he was inconsistent. Both criticize Locke for the halfhearted quality of his empiricism and each, in his own way, sought to thresh out the inconsistencies in Locke's philosophy.

Berkeley's finished philosophy is a curious mixture of empiricism and idealism. The overall purpose of his writing is highly apologetic in intent. He employs a rigorous empiricist critique of knowledge in order to confound the materialists and atheists of his age. This effort serves, in his view, to clear the way for his constructive project, namely, to prove the existence and providential nature of God, as well as the immortal nature of the soul. For our purposes, we will restrict our analysis to Berkeley's critique.

As we have observed, Locke affirmed the existence of an external, material world that is the direct and indirect cause of our sense impressions or ideas. On strict empiricist grounds, Berkeley attacked this affirmation as an utter non sequitur.

> It is indeed an opinion strangely prevailing amongst men, that houses, mountains, rivers, and in a word all sensible objects, have an existence, natural or real, distinct from their being perceived by the understanding. But with how great an assurance and acquiescence soever this principle may be entertained in the world, yet whoever shall find in his heart to call it in question may, if I mistake not, perceive it to involve a manifest contradiction. For what are the aforementioned objects but the things we perceive by sense? And what so we perceive besides our own ideas or sensations? And is it not plainly repugnant that any one of these or any combination of them should exist unperceived?[65]

With his fundamental principle, "to be is to be perceived" (*esse est percipi*), Berkeley sets out to unmask the illusory quality of the "common sense" bridge that Locke erects to link the ideal and the real orders of being. Berkeley consistently shows that, within the purview of empiricist principles, we only experience "phenomena" (bundles of sensible qualities or ideas) and never "noumena" (the purported objective causes of these qualities). Hence, it is not rationally justified to posit a material substratum as the causal ground of our phenomenal experience. As a corollary to this assertion, Locke's distinction between primary and secondary qualities becomes superfluous; for the former are no less dependent than the latter on perception. Berkeley writes: "In short, extension, figure, and motion, abstracted from all other qualities, are inconceivable. Where therefore the other sensible qualities are, there must these be also, to wit, in the mind and nowhere else."[66]

Building on Berkeley's critique, but without his idealist ends, Hume attempts to expound a thoroughgoing and consistent empiricist view of reality. As Maréchal writes: "A brief formula sums up all Hume's characteristics as a philosopher: he is a consistent empiricist right to the end."[67] Hume's ideal was to apply the experimental method, so successfully utilized by Newton in natural science, to the study of man. Human psychological processes and moral behavior must be approached inductively, and the empirical data gained in the process can serve as the basis of a truly scientific understanding of *Homo sapiens*.

When Hume inventories the contents of the mind, his terminology differs slightly from that of Locke. As we have noted, Locke vaguely terms all perceptions "ideas." Hume, however, asserts: "All the perceptions of the human mind resolve themselves into two distinct kinds, which I shall call impressions and ideas. The difference betwixt these consists in the degrees of force and liveliness with which they strike upon the mind, and make their way into our thought or consciousness."[68]

For Hume, "impressions" are the equivalent of "sensations," or that which is experienced immediately and directly. "Ideas" are copies, images, or representations employed in thinking or reasoning. "Complex ideas" can be dissected into simple, component ideas, and, in turn, "all our simple ideas proceed, either mediately or immediately, from their correspondent impressions."[69]

Thus, sense impressions are the immediate object of knowledge. But what is their source or origin? In responding to this question, Hume does not shrink from the rigor of empiricist logic, and frankly admits: "As to those impressions, which arise from the senses, their ultimate cause is, in my opinion, perfectly inexplicable by human reason, and 't will always be impossible to decide with certainty whether they arise immediately from the objects, or are produced by the creative power of the mind, or are derived from the author of our being."[70]

With this admission, Hume makes the logical leap to the position of skepticism that Maréchal finds implicit from the outset in the empiricist point of view. In accordance with empiricist epistemology, we are restricted to the confines of a subjective experience of the world and, on strictly empiricist grounds, we have no means of extricating ourselves from this web of subjectivity. According to Hume, we can provide a descriptive, psychological analysis of the cognitive habits by which impressions are transformed into simple ideas and these, in turn, are utilized to formulate complex ideas. We can also note how certain theoretical constructs are more useful than others, in that they enable us to make our way in the world more successfully. What we cannot do within the bounds of a consistent empiricism is to anchor our intellectual constructions in anything beyond what is given in immediate experience.

This series of conclusions is reflected in Hume's treatment of causality. Hume denies that it is either intuitively certain or capable of evident demonstration that whatever exists must have a cause for its existence. In Hume's view, all we can intuit are sensible phenomena. Thus, we may experience the fact that B has always followed A in the past, but such experience, by itself, does not justify the claim of a "necessary" causal connection between them. We only have impressions of one phenomenon following another, but there is no such thing as an impression of a causal relation.

But if the principle of causality is not a logical certainty on the basis of intuition or rational demonstration, how does it come to play such a vital role in our cognitive operations? Hume does not deny the centrality of causal relations in our thinking. He flatly states: "All reasoning concerning matters of fact seems to be founded on the relation of Cause and Effect. By means of that relation alone we can go beyond the evidence of our memory and senses."[71] But, as an empiricist, he asserts that causal relations refer to our *ideas* about objects and not to the objects themselves. Likewise, he believes he has shown that these relations are not logically necessary, nor do they arise from the mere experience of "phenomena." So he proceeds to explain the genesis of our causal claims in psychological terms. When A and B are constantly conjoined, this engenders the "habit" or "custom" of proposing a causal connection between them. Thus, custom supplants logic as the ground of inference.[72]

Hence, in Hume's view, we can and must continue to employ causal language if we are to make any sense out of our experience. For all practical purposes, this is an effective way of dealing with our world. But we must not delude ourselves into believing that such language has more than a psychological or sociological justification. If we are to remain true to empiricist principles, we must resist the temptation to go beyond these grounds and uncritically claim for it some kind of metaphysical warrant.

Hume engages this same unswerving empiricist logic in his treatment of the metaphysical status of the "self." There is, by his analysis, no direct impression of an enduring "self," and thus there can be no idea of such an entity that somehow undergirds and unifies the myriad individual impressions experienced throughout a lifetime. As Hume puts it: "For my part, when I enter most intimately into what I call my self, I always stumble on some particular perception or other. . . . I never catch myself at anytime without a perception, and never observe anything but the perception."[73]

True to the empiricist principle that ideas are derived from perceptions or impressions, Hume concludes that, as far as our *knowledge* goes, the human mind is "nothing but a bundle or collection of different perceptions, which succeed each other with inconceivable rapidity, and are in a perpetual flux and movement."[74]

In the appendix to the *Treatise*, Hume admits the inadequacy of his rendition of mind, and claims he was led to expound it only by "the seeming evidence of precedent reasonings." [75] His empiricism is based on the principles that all our impressions are distinct, and that the mind never perceives any real connection between them. If this is so, how are we to account for the "togetherness" of even that bundle of perceptions that constitutes Hume's minimal understanding of mind or self? Strictly speaking, on Hume's analysis, our mental life should be akin to a phantasmagoric array of unrelated impressions. Facing this difficulty, Hume states: "If perceptions are distinct existences, they form a whole only by being connected together. . . . But all my hopes vanish when I come to explain the principles that unite our successive perceptions in our thought consciousness." [76]

But this gaping discrepancy between his description of mind or "self" and our actual intellectual experience does not induce Hume to rethink or restructure his analysis in any radical way. Instead, he pleads the privilege of a skeptic, proclaims that the difficulty is not "insuperable," and looks forward to the time when "others, perhaps, or myself, upon more mature reflection, may discover some hypothesis that will reconcile these contradictions." [77]

In sum, Hume counsels us to adopt a moderate form of skepticism. Although it is the case that reason cannot provide a theoretical justification for our beliefs, we must, nonetheless, live, act, and make our way in the world. In Hume's view, a kind of natural belief in the validity of our mental operations, when bolstered by the dictates of custom, furnishes us with sufficient support as we go about our practical activities. As Hume affirms: "All these operations are a species of natural instincts, which no reasoning or process of thought and understanding is able either to produce or to prevent." [78]

What Maréchal's analysis shows is that Hume's phenomenalism is the polar opposite of Spinoza's rationalistic monism. Where Spinoza pursued the internal logic of Cartesian rationalism to the conclusion that it undercut the multiplicity of sense experience, Hume pursues the internal logic of empiricism to the conclusion that, in effect, it repudiates *any* theoretical foundation for the unity of knowledge produced by the intellect or understanding. As Maréchal puts it: "Empiricism pulverizes human knowledge; as a result it feels quite embarrassed before manifestations of unity which mischievous nature continually throws before it as so many obnoxious and insoluble problems."[79]

Maréchal concludes that empiricism, like rationalism, fails to resolve the antinomy between sense and understanding inherited by pre-Kantian philosophy from late medieval Scholasticism; both end in denying that sense and understanding can be brought into complementary interaction.

> On the road to empiricism, mere logic led to Hume's phenomenalism. On the road to ontologistic dogmatism or to rationalism, the same ruthless logic led to Spinoza's monism. The sceptical philosophy of Hume and the realistic philosophy of Spinoza represent, each in its own way, complete systems, terminal points for human thought. . . . Both of them also reveal the exact scope of the remote presuppositions which control them.[80]

According to Maréchal, it was Kant's great achievement to realize that both these philosophical approaches, when considered in themselves, represented dead ends for Western thought, from which, by their own isolated principles, no escape was possible. Consequently, Kant attempted to construct a critical synthesis of rationalism and empiricism that would salvage the partial truth that each contained, but also correct their deviations, so as to set Western philosophy once again on a fruitful course. Kant saw that the antinomy between sense and understanding, which plagued both rationalism and empiricism, must be overcome from a perspective that saw these faculties as operating in a unified, complementary fashion in the acquisition of knowledge. In the next chapter we will take up Maréchal's critical assessment of Kant's philosophical efforts, as well as those of his major successors.

CHAPTER THREE

Kant and the Post-Kantian Idealists

F
Immanuel Kant—
Intellect and Senses Rejoined

or Maréchal, the singular importance of Immanuel Kant's contribution to Western philosophy is his rediscovery of the need to postulate a synthetic relationship between the activities of sense and understanding if we are to construct an adequate account of the human power of cognition. As Maréchal sees it:

> The centuries-long conflict between dogmatic rationalism and empiricism was finally played out, during a period of about thirty years, in the midst of a thought that was honest, patient, rigorous and systematic. . . . The upshot was a partial solution to the fundamental antinomy of rationalism and empiricism. Since the two opposing tendencies had by then developed their most extreme consequences, Kant was able to reconcile them only by returning unconsciously to a synthetic viewpoint which had been overlooked by the ancestors of modern philosophy.[1]

Against the continental rationalists—with their emphasis on intellectual intuition and their concomitant denigration of sense experience—Kant defended the necessary role of sensation in the cognitive process. However, Kant also saw that a strictly empiricist analysis could not account for the unity and apparent necessity of our knowledge in fields such as mathematics and physics. Hence, Kant proclaimed:

> Experience is . . . the first product to which our understanding gives rise, in working up the raw material of sensible impressions. . . . Nevertheless, it is by no means the sole field to which our understanding is confined. Experience tells us, indeed, what is, but not that it must necessarily be so, and not otherwise. It therefore gives us no true universality. . . . Such universal modes of knowledge . . . must in themselves, independently of experience, be clear and certain. They are therefore entitled knowledge *a priori*; whereas, on the other hand, that which is borrowed solely from experience is, as we say, known only *a posteriori*, or empirically.[2]

Kant's major aim in the *Critique of Pure Reason* is to extract and elucidate the a priori element in our knowledge that reason itself supplies. He engages in what he calls "transcendental" analysis, which seeks the grounds or necessary conditions for the possibility of the knowledge we actually possess.

The empiricists had convinced Kant of the impossibility of portraying knowledge without a sensible component. But, for Kant, the mind did not just passively receive external stimuli; it *actively* shaped what it received in accordance with its own internal structures. The content of our knowledge stemmed from sense experience, but its form was imposed by the mind. This "form" represented the a priori element in knowledge. Thus, our knowledge is a synthesis of sensible and intellectual elements. Our sense experience was structured by a priori "forms" of intuition (space and time) and by the "categories" of the understanding (e.g., substance or cause): these a priori elements in the process of cognition organized our sense impressions into coherent objects of knowledge.

What is central for Kant is that knowledge cannot occur without the cooperation of sense and understanding, for they are inextricably interconnected; neither is subordinate to the other, for they both play necessary and complementary roles in our cognitive activity. The function of the categories is to synthesize or structure the data of sense intuition. They cannot be applied to realities that are not accessible to sense experience. Hence, any attempt to employ categories, such as cause or substance, to describe supersensible entities must be adjudged illegitimate. Consequently, from the point of view of pure or theoretical reason, our faculty of sense and intellection enable us to have mathematical and scientific knowledge of the world of "phenomena" (things as they appear to us), but these same faculties cannot be utilized to gain knowledge of the supersensible "noumena" (things-in-themselves).

Since this phenomena-noumena distinction figures so prominently in critiques of Kant, let us take a closer look at how Kant attempts to justify it:

> [The noumenon] is only the transcendental object; and by that is meant a something = X, of which we know, and with the present constitution of our understanding can know, nothing whatsoever, but which, as a correlate of the unity of apperception, can serve only for the unity of the manifold in sensible intuition. By means of this unity the understanding combines the manifold into the concept of an object.[3]

For Kant, the doctrine of the noumenon is a correlate of his doctrine of the transcendental unity of apperception. A glaring lacuna in Hume's empiricist analysis of mind is its inability to account for the unity of the intellectual experience of the individual thinker. Kant, however, asserts that we must postulate a transcendental unity of self-consciousness ("I think" must accompany all my representations) as a necessary condition for the cognitive experience we actually enjoy.[4]

In Kant's analysis, the transcendental unity of apperception is the primal, functional a priori principle in all human cognition, for neither sense perception nor intellectual synthesis is possible without it. More precisely, unless we assume a functional unity of consciousness, it would be nonsensical to speak of a sensible manifold being "thought" as objects of knowledge by means of the categories. Without this functional unity our cognitive experience could be nothing but a disjointed array of unrelated impressions.

Thus, Kant demonstrates that the integrated, rule-governed intellectual experience we undergo cannot be explained by a view of mind as a tabula rasa, but presupposes that the mind of the knower is a unified, active agent. Because, in Kant's view, this activity of mind does not extend to the *total* creation of the world of our experience, he is led to the necessity of positing the noumenon as a correlate of the transcendental unity of apperception. The appearances that are synthesized in the mind of the knower are appearances of something, namely, the noumenon or thing-in-itself (*Ding an sich*).

Maréchal defends Kant against the attack of thinkers like Friedrich Heinrich Jacobi, who claim that Kant's doctrine of the reality of the noumenon represents an unwarranted employment of the category of causality outside the phenomenal realm. According to Maréchal:

> The relation of the phenomenon to the "thing-in-itself" does not slip into the mind of Kant as a result of an illegitimate application of the category of causality as Jacobi and other opponents of integral Kantianism believed; the relation is imposed by the primordial law of reason as such: the law of necessary intelligibility of all that is posited by reason. To posit the phenomenon, is, by the same right, to posit the "thing-in-itself." [5]

Maréchal is asserting that what is operative in Kant's transcendental deduction of the noumenon is not the category of efficient causality but the principle of intelligibility or sufficient reason, as exercised by a dynamic intellect. Maréchal is thus not defending the Kantian phenomenon-noumenon split, for he rejects, as we will see, Kant's agnosticism vis-à-vis the noumenal realm. He is, however, supporting Kant's contention—against idealist critics—that our cognitive experience necessitates both a knower and an external reality which is independent of mind.

Thus, the affirmation of the noumenon is inextricably linked to Kant's whole theory of experience. Kant only wishes to assert that the subject endows experience with its formal structure. That things have to conform to the a priori conditions of the human subject in order to become objects of experience entails, for Kant, the idea of the "thing-in-itself," unrelated to the strictures of human cognition.

While Kant admits that we can say nothing positive about the noumenon or thing-in-itself, he maintains that the noumenon can have a legitimate negative sense, namely, as a "limiting concept," marking the boundaries of our sense-dependent form of knowledge, without ruling out the possibility of realities beyond those boundaries.

The concept of a noumenon is thus a merely *limiting concept*, the function of which is to curb the pretensions of sensibility; and it is therefore only a negative employment. At the same time it is no arbitrary invention; it is bound up with the limitation of sensibility, though it cannot affirm anything positive beyond the field of sensibility.[6]

Within the context of his system, Kant believes he has accomplished two things with his doctrine of the noumenon. First, he has ruled out traditional metaphysics, which purported to speak intelligibly about transempirical reality by applying the categories of the understanding to transcendent entities such as God or the soul. But, second, he has introduced the *possibility* of a supersensible, noumenal realm beyond the grasp of our discursive mode of apprehension.

Kant goes on to assert that we can affirm the existence of noumenal realities by a rational faith grounded in moral experience.[7] Indeed, speaking of his monumental efforts in the *Critique of Pure Reason*, Kant declares: "I have . . . found it necessary to deny *knowledge*, in order to make room for *faith.*"[8] Maréchal comments on this aspect of Kant's doctrine of the noumenon:

> To affirm [the noumenon], is to affirm that the object of knowledge is not necessarily exhausted by the phenomenon . . . it is to affirm the right to raise metaempirical problems, if not to resolve them speculatively. And one can see . . . from this moment, even without anticipating the further development of the Critique, how the philosopher could pride himself on not having dismantled reason, but on having directed it, by a rigorous reflection on itself, to recognize the inviolable domain of meta-empirical faith beyond the domain of rational science.[9]

Curiously, although Kant rules out traditional metaphysics, he nevertheless holds that the metaphysical urge is an ineradicable component of our mental life and has a vital role to play in our intellectual endeavors.

To delineate the proper cognitive function of the metaphysical urge, Kant distinguishes the intellectual activity of "reason" (*Vernunft*) from that of "understanding" (*Verstand*). If the categories of the understanding give unity to our experience of phenomena through the judgments they make possible, then the ideas of reason ("soul" as permanent ego, "world" as totality of causal relations, and "God" as the ultimate condition of all that is thinkable) can be seen as inspiring the search for ever greater insight into the nature of that unity, by directing our cognitive efforts toward their ultimate goal, namely, the "unconditioned." In Kant's own words, "the principle peculiar to reason in general, in its logical employment, is: to find for the conditioned knowledge obtained through the understanding the unconditioned whereby its unity is brought to completion." [10]

It is important to stress that, for Kant, these ideas of reason are neither innate nor gleaned from empirical data. They originate from the natural tendency of reason to complete the synthesizing activity of understanding. Unlike the categories of understanding, which are "constitutive" of the objects of our knowledge, the iedas of reason are merely "regulative" in nature. They direct the understanding to seek an ever-expanding and more comprehensive theoretical grasp of reality; they serve as ever-receding horizons of our unlimited desire to know.

Maréchal compares the regulative function of Kant's ideas of reason to the role of "theory" in contemporary scientific method.

Like the theoretical points of view of positive science, they [ideas of reason] are posited "hypothetically" by means of "problematic" concepts, and in this capacity they exert a directing and unifying influence over the content of our thought. . . . The hypothetical usage of the ideas of reason is thus similar to that of scientific theory: it is not so much knowledge but a "method," a "heuristic" procedure.[11]

Although we cannot employ the ideas of reason to extend our "theoretical" knowledge beyond the sphere of our phenomenal experience, we can affirm the reality of the transcendent referents of these ideas as postulates of "practical" reason.

These postulates are not theoretical dogmas but suppositions practically necessary; while then they do not extend our speculative knowledge, they give objective reality to the ideas of speculative reason in general (by means of their reference to what is practical), and give it a right to concepts, the possibility even of which it could not otherwise venture to affirm.[12]

Theoretical reason can neither prove nor disprove these postulates because they refer to entities outside the realm of possible experience; nonetheless, we should accept their reality on the basis of compelling practical interest. In such matters, Kant asserts that theoretical reason is subordinate to practical reason "since all interest is ultimately practical, and even that of speculative reason is conditional, and it is only in the practical enjoyment of reason that it is complete."[13]

Although Kant does not elaborate on the above statement, he seems to be arguing that the theoretical interest in "truth" is not, in itself, an absolute value. It must be integrated into the higher, practical search for the "good." The upshot of the doctrine of the primacy of practical reason is that we must hold to a set of affirmations by practical faith—even though they cannot be demonstrated theoretically—for without them the requirements of the moral life would be bereft of rational foundation. In this context, the following remarks of Etienne Gilson are illuminating:

> Failing a rational justification of morality, and granting that morality is inseparable from human life, there is nothing else to do but to take morality as a self-justifying fact. But when morality does not flow from what we know, it becomes free to prescribe for us what we ought to believe. . . . When, after cutting loose from metaphysics, ethics begins to dictate its own metaphysics, moralism appears upon the scene. The Kantian principle of the primacy of practical reason is a clear case of moralism, one of the classical escapes for those who despair of philosophy.[14]

In sum, Kant recognizes the primal, intellectual drive toward the absolute at the heart of our cognitive operations, but declares that any theoretical knowledge of this level of being is impossible. Thus, despite his defense of the reality of the soul and God as practical postulates of moral experience, he leaves the ideas of reason in a precarious state of epistemic limbo, reduced, as Hans Vaihinger would have it, to the status of "useful fictions"—to be held as if (*als ob*) they were true, simply because they support values that have practical utility.

Without theoretical justification, Kant's ideas of reason fall prey to the even harsher criticisms of the positivists, who have no taste for fictions, useful or otherwise, and whose solution is to banish the ideas of reason from serious consideration, as intellectual anachronisms from a credulous, pre-critical age. In their view, Kantian epistemology constricts the scope of our knowledge to the phenomenal realm, and we must be tough-minded enough to resist pietistic or moral longings that would seduce us into reintroducing theoretically unjustified metaphysical notions into our reckonings.

To be fair to Kant, he taught that theoretical reason could neither prove nor disprove anything with regard to the noumenal realm. The impossibility of theoretical falsification, when combined with positive practical motivations, seemed sufficient in Kant's eyes to warrant a rational faith in noumenal reality. Such a "soft" justification, which assumes an irremediable lack of ultimate integration between intellect and will, theory and practice, will always smack of "irrationalism" to those whose "ethics of belief" demand just such an integration.

Maréchal points out that Kant, who set out to overcome the antinomy of sense and understanding that tainted the legacies of empiricism and continental rationalism, ends by generating an antinomy of his own, namely, between understanding and reason. Within Kant's system, understanding is rigidly restricted to the bounds of the phenomenal realm, and the human intellect appears divided against itself. For Maréchal, reason (*Vernunft*) longs for more than the static, formal synthesis of sensible data that understanding (*Verstand*) provides, and it bridles at the limitation of its cognitive grasp to the appearances of an always imponderable noumenon or thing-in-itself. Practical reason informs us that our deepest moral strivings are grounded in the existence of noumenal realities, but understanding can properly offer no theoretical approach to these realities. Hence, within the scope of his system, Kant can only justify our ethical beliefs and practices by a nontheoretical moralism, which, in the end, presents a divided vision of our rational capacities.

Maréchal counts it to Kant's credit that he recovered the only way out of the impasse that beset modern philosophy; that is, he grasped the complementary roles of sense and understanding in the cognitive process. In some measure, then, the Kantian system marks an unwitting return to the Aristotelian-Thomistic doctrine of abstraction. As Maréchal remarks: "On both sides a contingent multiplicity, that is empirically acquired, is comprehended and universalized by a nonintuitive a priori of the intellect."[15] Both philosophical positions emphasize that, as embodied, finite creatures, all our knowledge begins with sense experience. Both assert that the mind is not merely a passive receptor of sense impressions but an active partner in structuring the data of sensation into an intelligible whole. Finally, both see that only when the joint contributions of sense and intellect are recognized, can we avoid stumbling into rationalist or empiricist caricatures of cognition.

However, Kant's failure to integrate the organizing function of understanding with reason's primal quest for the absolute foundations of knowledge led him to espouse a metaphysical agnosticism, from the point of view of theoretical reason, that is in stark contrast to the Aristotelian-Thomistic tradition. What lies behind Kant's failure in this regard? In his analysis of the a priori structure of knowledge, Kant identifies a hierarchy of transcendental conditions that are the logical prerequisites of the "objects" of cognition. Then, as Maréchal affirms, he appends to this hierarchy,

> by a necessary correlation with the transcendental unity of the "Ego," the pre-categorial affirmation of the "thing-in-itself," which represents, in the content of knowledge, an undetermined absolute, a negative noumenon, a genuine limit of the phenomenon, necessarily posited along with it, and thereby the true contact point [point d'attache] for the objectivity of our concepts.[16]

From Kant's perspective, to abandon the noumenon as the necessary correlate of the transcendental unity of apperception, and the phenomenon as appearance, would be to transmogrify his critical philosophy into an absolute idealism. We experience something external to us that cannot be reduced to internal states: our sensibility endows us with the capacity to be affected by this external reality under the a priori forms of space and time. This is why Kant, to the very end, staunchly held for an external reality independent of mind, against the criticisms of Jacobi, Fichte, and others. Hence, the doctrine of the "thing-in-itself" has a twofold function in Kant's system: (1) it anchors our experience in external reality; and (2) it forbids an uncritical identification of our experience of external reality as phenomenon with an experience of this reality's absolute, independent character as noumenon.

Maréchal points out that, like Kant, the Aristotelian-Thomistic tradition maintains the empirically based, discursive nature of the intellect. But, unlike Kant, this tradition does not thereby discount the very possibility of constructing an intelligible metaphysics. Maréchal believes that Kant erred in extending his justified repudiation of continental rationalism to the science of metaphysics in general. In fact, he holds that Kant's transcendental analysis need not have reached an agnostic conclusion vis-à-vis the possibility of metaphysical knowledge of the noumenal realm.

What does he [Kant] need to rejoin metaphysics in the full sense of the term? He obviously lacks the ability to apply certain formal determinations to the "thing-in-itself" besides its mere phenomenal expression; in other words, he lacks the ability to construct a system of positive noumena determined according to their own internal structure [en soi]. This inability is the result of the incomplete analysis Kant makes of the intellectual a priori which he places in synthesis with the empirical diversity. Kant did not see how the very a priori that makes the object of experience intelligible (by surrounding it with logical properties and projecting it toward a real absolute) must, in this objective function, ascribe to the absolute certain formal determinations at least of an analogical nature.[17]

Kant dismisses any theoretical determination of the nature of noumenal reality because he cannot conceive of its possibility, except when linked to direct intellectual intuition. In this regard, Maréchal feels that Kant does not totally escape the rationalist influence against which he was reacting.

If the former disciple of Leibniz and Wolff had detached himself from Cartesian Platonism to the point where he recognized the reciprocal causality of matter and form at the heart of our objective knowledge—which leads him closer to Aristotle—he nonetheless preserves, in the hypothetical conception he has of all ontology, something of the Platonic prejudice in favor of intuition.[18]

The touchstone of this Platonic prejudice is the belief that sense knowledge is relative and changing, and can at best achieve the level of opinion (*doxa*). Only pure intellectual intuition can arrive at a certain and immutable knowledge (*episteme*) of reality. Maréchal's point is that Kant did not liberate himself from the Platonic notion that *only* pure (nonsensuous) intellectual intuition can give us a true insight into the nature of reality; namely, provide us with a vision of the "thing-in-itself." Maréchal's goal is to expunge this rationalist remnant from Kant's thought, and, in so doing, to effect a rapprochement between Kantian analysis and the Aristotelian-Thomistic tradition. Maréchal sees this effort as a prolegomenon to devising a contemporary, post-Kantian metaphysics.

The very heart of Maréchal's enterprise is his attempt to demonstrate that a transcendental analysis of the a priori element, *without* appeal to a nonsensuous mode of intuition, reveals that a necessary affirmation of the noumenal absolute enters into the very constitution of every object of consciousness. Maréchal seeks to overcome the Kantian distinction between the understanding as "constitutive" of objects and reason as only "regulative" in nature. This, in turn, implies an undermining of the Kantian split between phenomenon and noumenon. In Maréchal's view, "knowing" (or better, "learning") is a fundamentally *dynamic* process by which we encounter, not merely appearances, but things-in-themselves precisely through their myriad appearances. Of course, the knowledge of things that we acquire by dint of our own efforts cannot be exhaustive; such total comprehension would involve knowing them sub specie aeternitatis, which is beyond our unaided finite intelligence. But our finite cognitive status—our grasp of reality being always partial and open to revision—does not warrant the Kantian phenomenon-noumenon split nor the accompanying assertion that we can know the former, but not the latter.

For Maréchal, the dynamism that animates our endless search for knowledge is the continuous human quest for the absolute. In his view, a properly conducted transcendental analysis of cognition will demonstrate that in every cognitive act we are implicitly seeking the ultimate ground of reality. Maréchal believes that this understanding of the fundamental "finality" of the intellect, and the implicit affirmation of the absolute in every act of cognition, can be linked with certain epistemological principles of the Aristotelian-Thomistic tradition to establish a viable and critical starting point for contemporary work in metaphysics. In chapter 4, we will follow Maréchal's efforts in this regard at length, but, before embarking on that sizable task, we must first review his treatment of post-Kantian idealism, especially in the person of Johann Gottlieb Fichte.[19]

From Critical Philosophy to Absolute Idealism

Despite their differences, Fichte, Schelling, and Hegel share the common concern of transforming Kant's critical philosophy into an absolute idealism. This metamorphosis requires the elimination of the "thing-in-itself," which, they agree, is a contradictory and unthinkable surd within the Kantian system.

As we have seen in Kant's analysis, the transcendental subject imparts structure to thought by means of the a priori forms of intuition and the categories of the understanding. The matter or raw material of cognition—that element not produced by the subject—comes from without, that is, from the thing-in-itself through the medium of sensation. To be sure, we can have no experience or knowledge of this raw material as such; it is only given to consciousness as *already* shaped by the a priori structures of the mind, but its existence is nonetheless a necessary logical correlate of the Kantian doctrine of the transcendental subject or unity of apperception.

It is this doctrine of the "thing-in-itself," this imponderable X, that is the focal point of the idealist attack on Kant. The post-Kantian idealists were in accord in asserting that Kant's own epistemological premises ruled out the possibility of such a mysterious entity, existing independently of mind. They believed that Kant's Copernican revolution in philosophy could finally be completed only by unflinchingly suppressing the thing-in-itself, thus recasting Kant's critical philosophy into a consistent idealism. As Maréchal writes, to these philosophers . . . the thing-in-itself appeared as an element of disharmony in the critical system; and since the deep root of this disharmony lay in the psychological dualism of the sensibility and the understanding, with its marked opposition between a material object of knowledge [matière de connaissance] and a knowing subject, the necessary corrective was self-evident: to derive the material object of knowledge from the subject itself.[20]

Of course, these idealists did not mean to derive the external world from the conscious or unconscious creativity of the finite human mind. Their intention was to transform the "transcendental" subject of Kant into an "absolute" subject that could serve as the basic metaphysical or ontological principle.[21]

In general, then, the post-Kantian idealists wanted to assert that the totality of reality (including, of course, the finite ego) represented the self-expression of absolute thought or reason. They wished to deny that there was any material substratum in the universe that was not, itself, the product and manifestation of thought or mind. As Fichte asserts: "No reality other than that of necessary thought falls . . . within the compass of philosophy."[22]

Given this fundamental metaphysical outlook, the post-Kantian idealists affirm that the unfolding of the cosmic process is systematic, intelligible, and teleological in nature. The world is a rational, coherent system directed toward a purpose, not a mechanistic series of events devoid of purpose. The goal of philosophy, then, is to be a rational reconstruction of the dynamic self-unfolding of absolute thought in all its phases of development. In this philosophical reconstruction, absolute thought reaches a reflective awareness of its own activity.

The post-Kantian idealists struggled to find an intellectual means to overcome the unreconciled division in Kant's thought that ruptured reality into phenomenal and noumenal realms, and that left the theoretical, moral, and aesthetic experience of humanity without internal rational coordination. Fichte, Schelling, and Hegel each sought to accomplish this task by transcending the subject-object (self-world) divide through an incorporation or synthesis of both halves of the duality in a metaphysical absolute that was their common ground and origin. Fichte strove to effect this synthesis from the point of view of moral experience, Schelling in terms of aesthetic experience, and Hegel from the perspective of logical experience, that is, the experience of thought itself. Fichte sets out to synthesize Kant's "pure" and "practical" reason. His goal is to develop a unified critique of reason as such. To do so, he must find a starting point, more primitive than Kant's, that coherently grounds both the speculative and moral functions of reason.

According to Fichte, if we inventory our experience or content of consciousness, we find that "[i]n brief, we may say that some of our presentations are accompanied by the feeling of freedom, others by the feeling of necessity."[23] If we consider many of our thoughts and actions—most notably, those with moral consequences—we do appear to create freely the world in which we live. We also undeniably experience the sheer "objectivity" or "facticity" of an external world that imposes itself inexorably upon us. At the outset of our philosophy, then, we must make a fateful decision either to explain the object in terms of the subject, which is creative thought and intelligence, or to objectify all subjective experience. As Fichte sees it, the former course leads to idealism; while the latter leads to dogmatism and, in the end, to a materialistic determinism that reduces intelligence to a mere epiphenomenon of physical processes. In Fichte's view, Kant does not squarely face the inevitability of this fundamental disjunction and thus seeks a middle way between idealism and dogmatism or materialism. The inconsistencies in Kant's system—such as his contention that human beings are phenomenally determined yet noumenally free—stem from his unwillingness to stand firmly on one side or the other of the idealism-dogmatism divide. For Fichte, a thinker who is aware of the primal freedom of the human being, as revealed in moral experience, will opt for idealism as the consistent means to explain material and spiritual reality in terms of creative thought or "intelligence-in-itself."

Kant believed in the validity of Newtonian (mechanistic) physics, and the *Critique of Pure Reason* represents a description of the structure of mind that accorded with this worldview; but he mistakenly assumed that his theoretical defense of causal determinism could be squared with the moral demand for freedom and the teleological thrust of organic life.

Fichte's attempt to reshape Kant's thought should thus be seen in the context of the Romantic defense of moral and artistic ideals against the ravages of mechanistic reductionism.[24] Kant's moralistic support of these ideals seemed halfhearted and artificial to Fichte. It had, therefore, to be supplanted by a full-scale metaphysical justification that grounded these ideals in the very nature of the macrocosmic creative process shaping the universe, of which human beings, through their creative endeavors, were microcosmic embodiments.

Like Kant, Fichte begins with the content of consciousness as a given, and, through reflection, strives to uncover the ground or conditions of its possibility. But, if he is to transform Kant's critical philosophy into idealism, he must push transcendental reflection beyond the Kantian starting point with its resultant dualities. According to Maréchal: "Fichte sees himself constrained, by his rigorous idealism, to infer an absolute principle which at once embraces the sensible given, the forms of space and time and the forms of pure reflection; furthermore, to be truly absolute, this principle must ground the speculative ego and the practical ego in a more radical unity."[25]

Fichte believed he had discovered this more primary starting point in the intellectual intuition of the pure ego as activity, striving, or internal dynamism (*Tathandlung*), which is presupposed in all our conscious operations.

> I cannot take a step, move hand or foot, without an intellectual intuition of my self-consciousness in these acts; only so do I know that *I* do it, only so do I distinguish my action, and myself therein, from the object of action before me. Whosoever ascribes an activity to himself, appeals to this intuition. The source of life is contained therein, and without it there is death.[26]

By this intuition of the pure ego, Fichte does not mean an esoteric, mystical experience; rather, transcendental reflection can reveal the pure ego as the nonobjectifiable ground of our very capacity for objectification.[27] It is thus the fundamental ground of the unity of consciousness.

Fichte's teaching in this regard can be clarified by contrasting it with Hume's empiricist approach to the "self." When

Hume peers into the mind, he claims to discover only distinct psychic states, the succession of which constitute the self, with no underlying unitive bond. But, unlike Fichte, Hume fails to see that the knower can only apprehend psychic phenomena through the objectifying activity of the self or subject, which cannot, itself, be objectified. For Fichte, "self" is always subject, never object. To be sure, one can engage in a reflexive act of self-analysis in which the "subject" is made into an object of scrutiny; but even this mental operation implies an intellectual activity which, itself, transcends objectification.

Kant, of course, denied that our discursive intellect possessed any capacity for intellectual intuition; he consequently attacked Fichte's claim to being a faithful continuator of his Copernican revolution in philosophy. Fichte, however, retorted that Kant had misunderstood the "object" of his intellectual intuition. We do not intuit the pure ego as a supersensible entity which transcends experience, but as an "activity" at the core of consciousness, uncovered through reflection. Furthermore, Fichte argued, Kant's own doctrine of the transcendental unity of apperception pointed in the direction of Fichtean intuition: the "pure ego as activity" was the transcendental ground of the logical operation of synthesis that the Kantian doctrine describes. Finally, in Fichte's view, Kant's categorical imperative was, itself, an intuition of the fundamentally active nature of the self or ego. As Maréchal contends:

> In the *Critique of Practical Reason*, Kant accepts the merchandise without the label: for what is the awareness of the categorical imperative if not intellectual intuition, certainly not of an immobile reality but of an autonomous act? All Kant would have needed, in order to join Fichte, was to know how to integrate the speculative and the moral domains in the fundamental intuition of the pure activity of the ego.[28]

Maréchal commends Fichte for having brought to light the dynamic structure of the intellect that undergirds its formal-logical operations. Fichte rightly emphasizes the dynamic finality of the primal intellectual striving, thereby integrating the theoretical and practical domains of knowledge in their very source or origin.

> A pure critical dynamism (Pure Ego) . . . is above all an "ought" (*sollen*) and, as a result, as soon as it adopts a formal content, it becomes the basis of a striving (*Streben*). . . . Fichte's interpretation brings the static transcendentalism of Kant to a necessary completion in so far as it restores activity, which signifies form, to its proper place.[29]

Fichte's phenomenology of consciousness accepts the necessity of positing a pure ego, understood as a fundamental striving or unlimited desire to know; but Fichte's idealist presuppositions require that he transform this phenomenological description into a metaphysical deduction. As an idealist, he is bent on deriving nature and all finite selves, insofar as they are objects of knowledge, from the side of the ego or subject. Since Fichte rejects solipsism—that the individual, finite self creates its own universe—he must then interpret the pure ego as a supraindividual, absolute ego, which produces the totality of reality, and which is reflected in finite consciousness.

At the finite level of human experience, there is a definite sense in which we do create our own world (*Lebenswelt*) through praxis. The world is not there for us an alien reality, but represents a field for our activity. In other words, we organize our world as a meaningful reality in the light of our practical or moral aims. In this context, the comments of William James are instructive:

> We may, if we like, by our reasonings unwind things back to that black and jointless continuity of space, and moving clouds of swarming atoms which science calls the only real world. But all the while the world we feel and live in will be that which our ancestors and we, by slowly cumulative strokes of choice, have extricated out of this, like sculptors, by simply rejecting certain portions of the given stuff.[30]

However, as finite creatures, one of our surest insights is that we do not create the world ex nihilo. In this sense, James's image of the sculptor is quite apt; for we work with an already given external reality that appears to have its own independent existence.

As we have already emphasized, Fichte, with his idealist presuppositions, cannot accept any reality that is independent of mind. He does not deny the fact of empirical consciousness that nature is independent of our individual, finite creative capacities, but he seeks to ground both human creativity and the external world in an all-encompassing metaphysical source that is spiritual rather than material in nature. And he can see no consistent means to that end except absolute idealism.

Fichte envisions the absolute ego as an infinite striving toward self-realization by means of free, moral activity. The absolute ego posits the nonego as the sphere in which this moral realization can be attained.[31] Because it does this spontaneously, below the level of consciousness, the role of the philosopher is to retrace its workings, consciously, through reflection.

In retrospect, then, both Kant and Fichte begin with the fact of human consciousness and seek, through transcendental analysis, to unearth its necessary grounds or conditions. Kant does not, however, think it possible to arrive at a single, totally unconditioned principle from which the entire content of consciousness can be derived. Kantian transcendental analysis of the forms of intuition and the categories of the understanding can account for the "form" that our knowledge takes, but it cannot totally account for its "content." The latter must, in some measure, be attributable to a reality existing independently of mind, namely, the thing-in-itself. Thus, in the end, Kantian epistemology remains dualist in character. By contrast, Fichte and his idealist successors assimilate finite human consciousness into an absolute thought or ego, and thereby seek an intelligible rendering of the totality of reality, including finite minds and nature, as a logical and coherent development of the primal absolute.

Maréchal lauds Fichte's recovery of the dynamic finality of the intellect, and his attempt to overcome the Kantian breach between theoretical and practical reason. He is nonetheless critical of the idealist assimilation of the finite and the infinite: "One can discern, without difficulty, the assumption concealed in this attempt: it cannot succeed unless the very movement of our objective reason, while constructing a 'rational system,' coincides completely with the movement of an absolute, creative thought."[32]

This assumption is at variance with Maréchal's Thomistic outlook, for "according to Thomism our thought reflects the absolute thought without entirely coinciding with it: whereas absolute thought is creative energy, ours is only an assimilative striving."[33] Despite the deductive virtuosity of the post-Kantian idealists, Maréchal opposes this assumption at the heart of their systematic enterprise as presumptuous and dogmatic. Furthermore, the monistic idealism it generates "goes far beyond the demand for unity inherent in our objectifying intellect."[34]

In the fifth volume of *Le Point de Départ*, Maréchal strives to show that we can employ the dynamic nature of the intellect as a basis for overcoming the deficiencies of Kantian analysis while remaining within the ambit of critical realism, thus rendering the flight to idealism unnecessary. He attempts to demonstrate that we can provide a post-Kantian metaphysical ground for the content of consciousness without subscribing to the idealist demand that "the entire content of consciousness must not only be interior to the subject, but proceed *exclusively* from the subject."[35]

Maréchal locates the dogmatic thrust of absolute idealism in its tendency to overestimate the capacity of finite human reason to fathom the ultimate nature of being, itself, and in its presumption that—at least in the person of the philosopher—the human mind can, by dint of its own labor, arrive at an absolute, definitive account of the logical necessity underlying the apparent contingencies of the world order. In this regard, idealism emulates the spirit of continental rationalism, with its assurance of the utter perspicacity of our "clear and distinct ideas." Both philosophical approaches seek a logical and coherent reconstruction of the world that flows, with a flawless deductive rigor, from an absolute and indubitable point of departure. To such a mind-set, the finite, sense-dependent, historically conditioned state of humanity must be transcended so that its vision of empirical reality can be revamped from an eternal, infinite perspective. In this context, James Collins makes the following pertinent remarks:

> Man is genuinely and radically finite, so that at no time in his development does he discover himself to be a phase in the self-explication of the absolute. Hence he cannot draw upon some creative idea implanted in his mind as its *a priori* structure on the strength of which an entire philosophical system can be developed

from the internal resources of the central idea. Kierkegaard requires a real rather than a dissimulated dependence of human intelligence upon the data of the physical world gained through the senses.[36]

Like Kierkegaard, Maréchal proclaims that idealist systems achieve their systematic ends by obliterating the distinction between God and the finite mind: "If it is incontestable that subsistant thought, the *Nous*, must be the universal principle of things and of minds, it does not seem that the active essence of our individual minds entirely coincides with this absolute, creative thought."[37]

What Maréchal desires, instead, is a "realist" metaphysics of creator and creature which demonstrates the immanence of the absolute in creation, without compromising its transcendence; he strives to show that the German idealist emphasis on the "dynamic" nature of the activity of thinking can be linked with certain insights from the Aristotelian-Thomistic tradition to undergird just such a metaphysics.

By way of summary, we can say that Maréchal commends Kant as a pivotal figure in Western philosophy because of his rediscovery of the synthetic nature of our intellectual life: cognition can only be conceived coherently when sensation and intellection are portrayed as complementary functions. He deplores, however, Kant's static view of intellection, which gives rise to his bifurcation of reality into phenomenal and noumenal realms, and of reason into theoretical and practical domains. The post-Kantian German idealists rightly pointed to the goal-directed dynamism that is the lifeblood of all intellectual striving, which even Kantian analysis tacitly presupposes. Unfortunately, they grafted this vital phenomenological insight onto a metaphysical structure that uncritically commingles finite and infinite perspectives.

In line with Kant, Maréchal's Transcendental Thomism enunciates a synthetic epistemology of "matter" and "form": the active capacities of the intellect structure the data given to consciousness via sensation. Like German idealism, Maréchal's philosophy proclaims that the rigid Kantian barriers which separate theoretical from practical reason, and the phenomenal from the noumenal object, dissolve once the dynamic nature of thinking is grasped; similarly, it envisions the ultimate driving force of all cognitive endeavors as the ongoing struggle to comprehend, in however inchoate a fashion, the absolute, unconditioned ground of reality. But Maréchal takes great care to delineate—as he believed idealists failed to do—the extent to which our unaided, finite rational capacities can achieve their ultimate, lofty end.

In turning finally to our exposition and analysis of Maréchal's Transcendental Thomism, we will address two critical questions: (1) Does Maréchal's position successfully avoid the pitfalls he has so artfully exposed in past systems? and (2) To what extent does Maréchal's Transcendental Thomism offer a viable defense of the pursuit of metaphysics?

CHAPTER FOUR

Beyond Kant

The Roots of Transcendental Thomism

I
*Comparison of Metaphysical and
Transcendental Critiques of Knowledge*

n the first four volumes of *Le Point de Départ*, Maréchal
makes the historical case that (1) the Aristotelian-Thomistic approach to epistemology is coherent and sound; (2) the
dissolution of this approach in late medieval philosophy generated insoluble epistemological conundrums that were the bane
of pre-Kantian modern philosophy; and (3) Kant reappropriated—however unwittingly—a portion of Aristotelian-
Thomistic epistemology; namely, the necessity of construing
the senses and the intellect as complementary vehicles in the
acquistion of knowledge. But the Kantian legacy is nonetheless
flawed and must undergo critical adjustment if epistemological
or metaphysical realism is once again to be vindicated.

In his fifth volume, *Le Thomisme devant la Philosophie Critique*, Maréchal pursues two fundamental lines of inquiry.

The first one, starting from the basic realism of direct and reflexive knowledge, will investigate knowledge itself as a totality of ontological relations between subject and object and discover in these ontological relations the logical characteristics of our various faculties. The second will first go along with Kant in order to proceed beyond him. It will reach the same conclusion which constituted the starting point of the first demonstration.[1]

Thus, Maréchal seeks to show that the metaphysical realism of the ancients can meet the critical demands of modern philosophy and that Kantian transcendental analysis, itself, contains an "implicit affirmation of a real metaphysical object."[2]

Maréchal distinguishes between a metaphysical critique of the object and a transcendental critique of the faculty of knowledge. The former was the philosophical vehicle chosen by the ancients, who, as objectivists, followed the mind's spontaneous impulse that "affirms at once the absolute reality of the object and only afterwards reexamines the latter, subdividing and organizing it in conformity with the strictest rules of analytic logic."[3] Ancient metaphysical realism sought, on the one hand, to justify the principle of identity and to defend objective affirmation against the challenge of skepticism, and on the other hand, to enunciate a synthetic understanding of conceptual knowledge that would overcome the apparent antinomy between sense and understanding, or being and becoming.

The metaphysical critique, therefore, accepts the ontological value of knowledge as given. It presupposes a natural relationship between thought and being; thus, the *quaestio de ponte* does not arise. There is simply no need to bridge a purported gap between the subjective experience of the knower and the objective reality of that which is known.

The transcendental critique, which takes shape in the thought of Kant, attempts to defend the reliability and validity of cognition through a radical analysis of the faculty of knowledge itself. To achieve this end, the transcendental critique proposes to go against the natural inclination of the mind, by suspending its primal drive toward the objective affirmation of that which it "knows," in order to delimit and examine the content of our consciousness, thereby seeking to discover those conditions which constitute objects of knowledge. As Maréchal puts it: "For the transcendental critique interest is at first wholly concentrated upon the internal genesis of the object as object, upon the *'fieri'* of the immanent object insofar as this *'fieri*,' far from being only a succession of psychological moments, contains the absolute and universal conditions of the possibility of the objects in general."[4]

According to Kant, transcendental reflection upon the content of consciousness reveals the "unified diversity" of the objects of knowledge therein contained. More precisely, material diversity, which is the product of sensation, is unified in our consciousness according to formal conditions that are a priori, in that they cannot be derived from sensation as such. The transcendental method does not merely seek the a priori conditions of the possibility of any particular object, but the universal, necessary conditions of every possible object of a discursive (nonintuitive) intellect.

Thus, Kant's transcendental method and his Copernican revolution in philosophy turn on the contribution of the subject to the construction of the objects of knowledge. But what is the precise nature of this subject's activity? Kant correctly saw that knowledge is the result of a synthetic interaction of sense and understanding, which stand to one another in a relationship of matter to form. But, according to Maréchal, the mistake to which Kant succumbs is to interpret the "form-giving," "unifying" role of the understanding in static rather than dynamic terms.

The form that understanding contributes to knowledge must not be viewed as an "immobile wrapping around some matter,"[5] but as "the activity by which the matter of knowledge is actively informed by the internal finality, by the natural becoming of the subject."[6] In other words, our concepts or objective representations, and the a priori structures of the mind that help constitute them, must not be isolated from the primal thrust of the intellect toward being.

Maréchal contends that Kant, in his *Critique of Pure Reason*, falls back on an abstract and rigid conception of "form" in the spirit of Cartesian rationalism. As a result, Kant portrays the transcendental unity of apperception and the categorical functions as a kind of logical filter through which sense impressions must mechanistically flow in order to emerge as objects of experience. This mechanistic conception of mind fails to unearth the primal human drive to know being, in which our

cognitive and volitional capacities converge, and which underlies and animates all our logical operations. Hence, what Kant
offers is a truncated account of cognition that does not penetrate below the surface of our logical-synthesizing abilities to
their origin in our unique character as knowing, willing, and
feeling agents.

Maréchal seeks to remedy this flaw by demonstrating that
the transcendental method, when properly portrayed, presupposes

> that in reflection our objective concepts are given to us as active
> determinations of some assimilated matter, as a passing from an
> objective potency of determination to actual determination, as the
> immanent "movement" of a knowing faculty as such. Besides, it is
> only on this condition that the transcendental critique of the object
> would really constitute, as Kant claims, a "critique of the power of
> knowledge" not simply an abstractive analysis of the object.[7]

For Maréchal, a thoroughgoing transcendental analysis of
the content of consciousness, unencumbered by the rationalist
presuppositions that stifled Kant, reveals the unifying power of
a "subject in act" at the heart of our cognitive operations. Maréchal believes that, once the dynamic nature of cognition has
been realized, he can further show that "the transcendental critique would be legitimately completed only by the rational admission of finality which reveals to us the existence of an
Absolute Being. Kant, the patient pioneer, would be completed
rather than contradicted."[8]

Kant recognizes the fundamental drive of the human intellect toward the absolute or unconditioned as the ground of the
ideas of reason. But he maintains that, since the absolute is not
an object of direct experience, and since the categories of the
understanding can only legitimately synthesize experience-
based data, the mind's admitted dynamism toward the absolute
can play a "regulative," but not a "constitutive," role in the cognitive process. Thus, if Maréchal is to succeed in completing
Kant's enterprise, if he is to demonstrate a convergence between the metaphysical and transcendental critiques as the
foundation of his own Transcendental Thomism, he must
show that Kant's appraisal of the role of this dynamism is un-
necessarily restrictive. And if, in the process, Maréchal is to

avoid slipping into ontologism, he must demonstrate that this dynamism gives us access to the noumenal or metaempirical realm and has a "constitutive" role in cognition, without appealing to an immediate intuition of the metaphysical absolute.

Aquinas's Metaphysical Critique

Maréchal wishes to indicate that the metaphysical critique of knowledge embodied in the work of Thomas Aquinas can be justified in the light of Kantian criticism. To do so, he must show that Aquinas's confidence in the metaphysical value of knowledge was neither philosophically naive nor gratuitous.

In good Aristotelian fashion, Aquinas engages in his own brand of philosophical doubt. He arrests the mind's spontaneous affirmation of being to discover whether it is warranted in the light of skeptical protest.[9] As Maréchal explains, Aquinas's metaphysics has a critical, rather than a dogmatic, starting point in that it does not encourage a naive or unreflective affirmation of the correspondence between thought and being.

> Is this not also, in a very exact sense, the critical attitude of the entire modern critique of knowledge? The critique can lead to . . . scepticism as well as to affirmation: but it always begins with an entirely detached and totally provisional consideration of the spontaneous activity of the mind: universal, methodic and provisional doubt concerning the absolute object of our thought.[10]

The methodic doubt of Aquinas can be compared to that of Descartes, who engaged in a radical and extensive mode of doubting, with a view toward arriving at a self-evident and indubitable ground upon which to reconstruct philosophy systematically. By this process, Descartes came to the isolated ontological ego (*res cogitans*), from which he could not emerge without the aid of a theological escape. Aquinas, however, urges us to employ reflective reason to suspend momentarily our spontaneous affirmation of the object of knowledge, and withhold judgment, until we have impartially weighed the possibility of universal doubt or skepticism. According to Maréchal:

The purpose of St. Thomas is not, as with Descartes, to reach, as soon as possible, among all other possible "truths" a privileged one, which is indubitable, well defined and capable of serving as a constructive starting point. His intention is not so particularized; the scope of his doubt is wider and, paradoxical though it may sound, it is more thoroughly "modern" for it aims at nothing less than setting up a general critique of truth as such.[11]

Thomistic methodic doubt, unlike its Cartesian counterpart, does not seek an escape from the flux of sense-dependent knowledge through the achievement of an intuitive certainty that artificially ignores our actual being in the world. Rather, it aims at discovering whether beings like ourselves, with our earth-bound facticity, can arrive at truth through the employment of our discursive cognitive faculties.

According to Aquinas, absolute doubt is not possible because reflection reveals "that it is self-evident that there is truth in general . . . for he who denies its existence, grants that truth exists; for if truth does not exist, it is true that truth does not exist: but if something is true, the truth must exist."[12]

Maréchal discovers a transcendental necessity in Aquinas's reasoning; namely, "the relation of truth is inherent in objective thought, for, if denied, it surges again from the very negation."[13] Since even the denial of truth implies its affirmation, and since a supposed neutrality on the issue of truth in general can be unmasked as illusory, we see that thought ineluctably posits a relation to truth.[14]

Maréchal takes this transcendental relation of thought and truth as indicating the impossibility of a purely subjectivist epistemology. Thought is inevitably projected toward an external criterion or pole, namely, being. But, if being is to serve as an effective external norm for thought, then the two must be linked in a determinate relationship. The "principle of identity" provides such a link, for it guarantees the fundamental stability both of our mental operations and of the being to which these operations are related.

At the core of relativism (whether ancient or modern) is the contention that, although the principle of identity may be a necessary first principle of thought, it cannot for that reason be assumed to be a necessary law of external reality. Against such a position Maréchal must show that the principle of identity could not be normative for thought without serving the same function for reality as well.

To this end, Maréchal asks, with Aquinas, "whether the intelligible species abstracted from the phantasm is related to our intellect as that which is understood."[15] At issue is whether our concepts are the means by which we gain direct knowledge of the external world (*id quo intelligitur*) or are, themselves, the object our knowledge. If the latter is the case, then, according to Aquinas, sheer relativism is introduced into the cognitive order; for if our intellectual faculties only give us knowledge of our own internal states, then contradictories (A and not A) may be simultaneously true for different people, or for the same person at different times. Such a state of affairs would surely cut off the possibility for logically coherent thought and discourse. As Maréchal notes:

> To condemn pure relativism in the domain of knowledge in the name of the first principle, is first of all to observe, without doubt, that this relativism makes all expression of thought illusory; because, in the absence of an absolute norm external to individual thought, the most openly self-contradictory statements would be equally legitimate.[16]

That our knowledge of the world at any particular time is inevitably suffused with a degree of relativity and incompleteness is a necessary correlate of the cognitive limitations inherent in our finite status. But it does not follow from this admission that the intellectual domain is in a continual whirl. Despite paradigm shifts that generate differing theories to explain the complex workings of the universe, our underlying ability to classify the contents of the world intelligibly in terms of specific, natural kinds remains constant. Without this capacity, our experience would indeed be a nightmarish jumble. Hence, the operation by which we grasp an individual object as a thing of some specific sort is at the heart of the cognitive process. Following Aristotle, Aquinas calls the ability to comprehend the particular under a general concept "abstraction."

Through the medium of sensation we are immersed in the world around us. This immediate sense contact with external objects is a fundamental characteristic of our being in the world. But sense contact alone, without intellectual intervention, would amount to total abandonment to the world. We achieve a rationally coherent view of external reality only by distinguishing ourselves, as knowing subjects, from the other myriad objects to be known. Because the intellect has no independent, intuitive knowledge of the world, it must turn to the images that result from the contact between the world and our senses.[17] The intellect (*intellectus agens*) then abstracts the universal form of the object under consideration from the particularizing material elements that render it an individual thing.

But we must not conclude that the resultant concept (*species*), considered merely as a modification of the mind, is the object of thought. "By its very definition the *species* as such is but an accidental modality of our cognitive activity."[18] In this context, the following comment by Bernard Lonergan is helpful:

> It is plain that phantasms are illuminated, immaterialized, universalized in act. Aquinas said so repeatedly. More precisely, it is phantasm, not in the sense of act of the imagination, but in the sense of what is imagined, that is illuminated; for what is illuminated is what will be known; and certainly insights into phantasms are not insights into the nature of acts of imagination but insights into the nature of what imagination presents.[19]

In other words, our classification of the world into natural kinds is not an isolated mental or logical enterprise, but arises from, and is founded in, our contact with the world (*fundata in re*). Thought is not directed to itself but to being. Hence, our root ability to make sense out of the world necessitates that the first principle (the principle of identity) be both logically and ontologically valid.[20]

Thus, from the Thomistic point of view, the problem of discovering a bridge between the ideal and the real, or the logical and the ontological, is a pseudoproblem. It rests on the mistaken assumption that conceptual knowledge can originate in other than a sense-dependent and world-related fashion. From this perspective, Descartes's *res cogitans*—an isolated mind thinking its own thoughts, severed from the world that is its natural home—has the look of an intellectual artifice, one that has, unfortunately, generated a host of insoluble dilemmas in Western thought. But when we look at these dilemmas from a Thomist perspective, they disappear. Marjorie Grene explains: "My awareness is not a separate subjective 'in-itself,' but at one and the same time an assimilation of what is beyond and an extension of myself into the things beyond. This interpenetration of 'self' and 'world' is not only a central characteristic of mind; it is what mind is."[21]

In our interlocking universe no element exists in isolation; rather, every element is in a continual state of interaction with its environment. What, however, is the nature of our interaction with the universe such that it results in our knowledge of external objects? How is it possible for us to transform the effects of other beings upon us into a knowledge of those very beings?

It cannot be overemphasized that, in the Aristotelian-Thomistic framework, knowledge is not merely a passive reflection of the object in the subject. Rather, knowledge is an achievement, the end result of an activity or striving on the part of the subject. As Maréchal puts it, "The object will be the immanent term of the subject's activity only to the extent that it will have inserted itself among the dynamic conditions of the subjective activity."[22] The *species* or form is the means by which the external object is immanent in the subject.[23]

The human mind exists in an openness to know all that it encounters (*potens omnia fieri*). In principle, then, everything that "is," is potentially intelligible or knowable. Mentally speaking, I am what I know. Correlatively, from the perspective of the object, it is in the human activity of knowing that its potential intelligibility becomes realized. In Scholastic parlance, an object that was intelligible in potency (*in potentia*) becomes intelligible in act (*in actu*) in the process of intellection. Thus, Aquinas asserts: "The intellect and what is understood are the same,"[24] or, in another instance, "The thing understood is the perfection of the one who understands."[25] Accordingly, what distinguishes a "knowing" being is this capacity to effect an epistemic linkage with the "other" while still remaining itself. This union of the knower and the known, which is the centerpiece of the Aristotelian-Thomistic doctrine of cognition, cannot involve the obliteration of their separate identities, for this would undermine the subject-object distinction that is the foundation of discursive consciousness. Consequently, this union cannot be conceived in material terms, but must be immaterial in nature. On this point, Aquinas writes:

> Knowing beings are distinguished from non-knowing beings in that the latter possess only their own form, while the knowing being is naturally adapted to have also the form of some other thing; for the *species* of the thing known is in the knower. . . . Now the contraction of the form comes from matter. Hence . . . forms according as they are more immaterial, approach more nearly to a kind of infinity. Therefore, it is clear that the immateriality of a thing is the reason why it is cognitive, and the mode of knowledge is immateriality.[26]

Of course, Aquinas is not here denying that our earthbound human mode of cognition necessarily contains a vital, material-physical component. His central epistemological tenet is that knowledge is the achievement of the total human person, as a composite of mind (soul) and body in which both play indispensable complementary roles. The acquisition of knowledge is unquestionably dependent on the proper organic functioning of the senses and the brain as necessary conditions; but, in Aquinas's view, such merely physical processes could not constitute a sufficient condition to effect the intimate union of knower and known which we call knowledge. Conscious mental activity cannot be explained adequately as a discharge and transfer of material atoms from the object to the soul, as Democritus taught, nor, to use more contemporary terms, as the epiphenomenon of an intricate concatenation of neuro-physiological events. Aquinas teaches that an adequate account of human cognition requires that we develop an understanding of the intellect that transcends the confines of naturalism. Hence, he depicts the functioning of the intellect within the human person as a nonmaterial or spiritual process that operates in concert with the mechanisms of the body.[27]

The Aristotelian-Thomistic tradition views the intellect as both active and passive in nature. The active power of the intellect (agent intellect) is capable of abstracting the intelligible from the sensible. When we are confronted by a particular object, the senses provide us with a whole gamut of visual, auditory, tactile, gustatory, and olfactory information. This information is synthesized in the imagination, and thus arises a likeness (*similitudo rei particularis*) or image of the particular object. For Aquinas, sensation is the focal point of our dynamic interaction with the world. The receptive potentiality of our senses is actualized by contact with external objects. But sensation can only inform us about the external or accidental qualities of objects (color, size, shape, etc.); it cannot penetrate to their essence, form, or intelligible structure. This latter task is the province of the agent intellect.[28]

The doctrine of the agent intellect is the Aristotelian-Thomistic attempt to explain how our contact with particular entities through sense experience can be transformed into conceptual knowledge of universals. Both Aristotle and Aquinas view the intellect as partially passive in nature, in that it is open to receive information from all that it encounters. As Maréchal explains: "Our intellectual faculty contains a certain internal passivity in the sense at least that it is not always in the act of knowing, and only passes from potency to act in the presence of a phantasm and in accordance with its representative content."[29]

Aristotle called this "passive" side of our intellectual faculty the "possible intellect," to distinguish it from an intuitive intellect of the Platonic type which would have direct insight into the intelligibility of things. Plato taught that we could rise above the uncertainties of sense experience and achieve an intuitive insight into the transcendent universal forms, ideas, or exemplars, of which particular material entities were imperfect replicas. Aristotle, however, rejected the independent existence of such universal forms; in his view, forms exist *only* as particular material entities in the world. He likewise denied any capacity for a direct, intuitive grasp of reality that could bypass the senses. For Aristotle, our intellect is passive vis-à-vis the world to the extent that it must be energized by an external determination whose origin lies ultimately in our sense contact with the world.

Now, having presented the basic framework of the Aristotelian-Thomistic epistemology, we must proceed to a detailed analysis of the process of abstraction, which represents the cornerstone of our cognitive experience.

The Process of Abstraction

Aristotelian-Thomistic epistemology teaches that the agent intellect renders potentially intelligible images of individual entities actually intelligible by a process it calls "abstraction." According to Aquinas: "The agent intellect abstracts the intelligible *species* from the phantasm since by the power of the agent intellect we are able to take into consideration, apart from individual conditions, the nature of *species*."[30]

The agent intellect has the capacity to distinguish the essence or form of the object under scrutiny from the individuating material aspects contained in the image. Hence, when presented with images of three individuals, say, Paul, John, and Mary, whose physical appearances may differ considerably because of gender, race, and ethnic origin, we are not dumbfounded by their differences, but are easily able to classify them as members of the species *Homo sapiens*. Yet, those with a bent for abstract thought will want to discover the ground of this primal cognitive power in both the objects that we know and the mind of the knower. In technical terms, it is the search for a philosophical warrant for our confident and efficient use of logical universals to sort out, and make sense of, our experience.

We might reconstruct the logic of the Aristotelian-Thomistic argument for the existence of agent intellect and the process of abstraction as follows. Intelligibility is not possible without universality (universality is a necessary condition of intelligibility). What is given to us in sensation is particularized and individual. Hence, we must posit some spontaneous or active capacity of mind, capable of abstracting the universal component from the particularity of the objects of sense experience, as an a priori condition for the possibility of our cognitive experience. As Karl Rahner puts the matter:

The agent intellect is introduced again and again in Thomas as the *a priori* condition, inherent in thought itself, of the possibility of something actually intelligible, which actual intelligible as such is not found in sensibility, and according to the evidence of experience does not come to man from elsewhere.[31]

Nominalists of whatever vintage, in one way or another, argue that this logical or conceptual capacity requires no further grounding beyond the natural similarity or "family resemblance" among the individual things that we encounter. The critical or moderate realist responds that nominalism in its various manifestations inevitably "begs the question" as to the source of that similarity.[32] Furthermore, we will search in vain for a single identical "physical" characteristic that each member of a class must have so that we may adjudge it a bona fide member of that class. Hence, a thinker like Aquinas is led to postulate a metaphysical form or essence that binds the individual members of a class or kind, and that serves as the foundation in reality (*fundamentum in re*) for our universal concepts.

Let's look at the issue from another angle. A definition is a logical production of the mind, an abstract description that presumably captures something of the essence of an element of reality. At least since Wittgenstein, we have realized that providing strict definitions that apply to all members of a class is a tricky business. The best we might attain is a cluster of similar descriptions loosely connected by a kinship Wittgenstein calls "family resemblance."

Surely our capacity to distinguish horses from nonhorses is not dependent on any description, or cluster of descriptions, of "horse" that we can construct. Is not our actual cognitive experience one in which our ability to sort reality into classes is based on a kind of pre-logical awareness of natural kinds existing in reality? Therefore, natural terms (universals) such as "horse" are rigid and indexical, pointing directly to the realities named, without being mediated by a second-order logical operation like a definition. In Scholastic language, it is our capacity to gain insight into the phantasm, by the power of agent intellect, to abstract the universal form from its individuating material elements that, in the first instance, makes the world intelligible to us.

Some contemporary philosophers writing in the Anglo-American tradition are likewise dissatisfied with the inadequacy of the nominalist account, and are also seeking a foundation in reality for our universal concepts. They expect such a foundation will rest on a primal level of physical analysis, which rigorous scientific investigation might eventually provide. In this context, D. M. Armstrong writes:

> But how is it determined when we have arrived at genuine generic identities? It is argued that we have nowhere to begin but with the classifications which we naturally make. Natural science may then take us beyond these classifications to more deeply hidden classings and sortings which, it is our hope, approach more closely to an isolation of genuine universals.[33]

For Aquinas, however, the *fundamentum in re* for universal concepts cannot be discovered at the material-physical level. In his view, matter is the principle of "individuation," accounting for the distinctiveness of individual entities. Consequently, it cannot account for their similarity as well. Aquinas, along with other medieval moderate realists, came to the conclusion that it is necessary to posit a metaphysical form or essence as a ground or a priori condition of our conceptualizing capacity because neither logic nor physics (alone or in tandem) could do the matter justice. John F. Boler gives us an important insight into scholastic methodology on this and other issues.

> It seems to me that one of the strong points of scholastic method is just that when it lacked ostensible "things" to account for a solution, it generally proceeded by refining the problem. The failure to grasp the significance of such an approach has led both critics and defenders to present unfortunate caricatures of medieval thought.[34]

In this case, the refining process led Aquinas to formulate an acute analysis of the origin of our distinctively human brand of conceptual knowledge. It caused him to reject an account of this knowledge in terms of logic or physics alone. For Aquinas, it is only by positing a metaphysical form inherent in each individual substance, as well as an active capacity of mind capable of intellectually abstracting that form from its individualized material embodiment, that we could make philosophical sense out of the knowledge we actually possess. To focus more sharply on what Aquinas actually means by abstraction, let us consider the following passage:

> The phantasm is both illuminated by the agent intellect and, beyond this, the intelligible *species* is abstracted from it by the power of the agent intellect. The agent intellect illuminates the phantasm because just as the sensitive part acquires a greater power by its conjunction with the intellect, so by the power of the agent intellect the phantasms are made more fit for the abstraction from them of intelligible intentions.[35]

If we are to construe properly the Thomistic doctrine of abstraction and the resultant intelligible *species*, we must scrupulously avoid the tendency to think of the intelligible *species* as a sublimated intellectual image of a "thing" in general, such as a "horse," "table," or "human being." Since, according to Aristotelian-Thomistic ontology, only individual entities exist, the mind can only contain particular, specific images, not images in general. Furthermore, as Maréchal contends, to interpret the intelligible *species* as a generalized image would rupture the continuous collaboration of sense and intellect in the cognitive process that Aristotelian-Thomistic epistemology consistently espouses. If we erroneously take the intelligible *species* as a generalized intellectual image, then

> once the *species* is in the possible intellect, such a collaboration would become superfluous since the *species* would intelligibly represent by itself all that the image represents on the sense level. But, according to St. Thomas, not only no single primary act of intellection, but also no use whatever of the *species* is possible except in the presence of the phantasm.[36]

To comprehend his epistemology correctly, we must not lose sight of the fact that, for Aquinas, our embodied, sense-dependent state dictates that all our knowledge—from what we know of the most elemental entities to what we naturally know of God—is necessarily linked to the images that result from sense experience. "Images necessarily accompany our knowledge in the present life, however spiritual the knowledge may be: for even God is known by us through images of his effects."[37]

Hence, the activity of agent intellect in the process of abstraction does not transport us directly beyond the sensible realm to a kind of "intuitive look" at ideal or metaphysical objects; rather, it enables us, while remaining firmly wedded to a particular image, to conceive that this image contains a form that is common to many. Thus, according to Maréchal, the intelligible *species* is better understood as a dynamic attitude toward the particular image or phantasm that uncovers its universality and, hence, its intelligibility.

> The *species* is by itself only a dynamic disposition of the intellect, qualitatively diversified in function of the phantasm. Thus the intelligible *species* never enters consciousness alone, like a complete intellectual representation which screens off the sense representation, but always according to a dynamic relation to the actual phantasm.[38]

But how is the agent intellect able to generate this attitude toward the phantasm, by which it discovers the universal in the particular? What is the origin of this vital intellectual operation, on which the entire edifice of human cognition is constructed? How does the intelligible unity of our conceptual life emerge from the diversity of our sense experience?

We can begin our approach to this difficult issue by agreeing that to render a state of affairs "intelligible" is to discover "unity" in diversity. Discrete particulars remain unintelligible until we find the common bond that unites them. But, as Maréchal points out, the human quest for intelligibility does not cease when we have uncovered the unity of species or natural kind. We then struggle to unite species into genera and so on *ad infinitum*.[39] Hence, the innate drive for intelligibility transcends any partial and relative unification we might achieve, and tends toward a total and absolute vision of the unity of being as such. Maréchal sees this intellectual quest for absolute unity as the driving force, and necessary precondition for, the relative degrees of unity and intelligibility we seek to find in all our separate cognitive operations. Thus, he writes: "But what is ultimately referred to the phantasm, and projected upon it as a phosphorescent screen which becomes luminous at the points of impact? To this question we shall answer in a word that the higher term of the relation imposed upon the phantasm by the intellect is the speculative unity of being."[40]

Maréchal believes that a proper understanding of Aquinas's account of cognition demonstrates the teleological thrust of the human quest for knowledge. The pure desire to know is limitless and oriented toward the absolute. This orientation is mirrored in every intellectual operation as the ultimate purpose (telos) which underlies and motivates our particular and immediate cognitive ends.[41] Furthermore, Maréchal sees our drive toward the absolute unity and intelligibility of being as a "constitutive," and not merely a "regulative," factor in our cognitive experience.[42]

As previously stated, to know or render something intelligible is initially to be able to classify it as a specific "kind" of thing. This presupposes the ability to distinguish its "form" or "essence" from its material concretion in the particular example under consideration. In Thomistic language, it involves the power of the agent intellect to recognize a form as limited by its material embodiment in an individual object.

Now, we can know a limit as "limit" only by being beyond it in some sense. Thus, for example, we can only identify an animal as a horse—that is, as a particular and limited representative of a species—if, in some way, we are already aware that the essence of "horseness" is wider than its concretion in this particular horse.[43]

To know any entity as "particular" and "limited" implies a broader horizon against which we consider it. Hence, the process of abstraction at the heart of our cognitive operations is only possible because of the agent intellect's capacity to view material objects against the background of the unlimited nature of their forms. But the horizon of the human intellect is not restricted to the recognition of the "unity of species." In fact, no finite level of unity or intelligibility can satisfy the intellect's longing for ever greater comprehension; thus, it experiences all its achievements as limited in nature. For Maréchal, this experience is only possible if the intellect has an inchoate grasp of its unbounded scope—its fundamental orientation to the absolute. He concludes that our "objectification" of our experience must be seen against the background of this fundamental orientation. In Maréchal's words: "Considered as a moment in the intellect's ascent towards the final possession of the absolute 'truth,' which is the spirit's 'good,' it implicitly projects the particular data in the perspective of this ultimate end, and by so doing objectivates them before the subject."[44]

It is important to realize that Maréchal is not referring to any *intuitive* insight into the absolute that bypasses the normal functioning of discursive reason. Rather, in his analysis, our drive toward the absolute is an integral, constitutive factor in the incremental process of human knowing. Following Aquinas, Maréchal holds that the final end of all intellectual activity—that which alone could satisfy its infinite longing—is an intellectual assimilation with the absolute. Although we cannot achieve this end in our finite, natural condition, it nonetheless inspires all our intellectual operations and grounds our unlimited desire to know. He writes that "every particular volition is inspired by the natural volition of the last end. Hence no activity of our intellect, no intellectual assimilation is possible but in virtue of the deep yearning whose saturating end would be the intuition of the absolute real."[45]

Two issues need to be clarified if we are to view Maréchal's position in proper perspective. First, the primal sense of "limitedness" that we experience when we encounter individual entities is not "physical" but "metaphysical" in nature. The entities may be limited in size, weight, etc., but more fundamentally they are limited in "being." We are intellectually driven to understand all entities we confront in terms of ever-broadening horizons because we apprehend the contingent nature of their being; that is to say, their existence is not independent or self-explanatory but only intelligible in terms of an indefinite number of other, related entities. In fact, contemporary physics tells us that we must conceive the universe as an organic whole in which each individual can only be rightly understood when viewed against the background of the totality.[46]

The universe can legitimately be called "limited" in the sense that it is contingent rather than necessary in being; that is, its very existence begs for an explanation in terms of some higher level of being. In the final analysis, it is this fundamental orientation that leads the mind to recognize the restricted nature of the beings that come within its purview, and impels it to relate them to ever more comprehensive explanatory schemes. Accordingly, for Maréchal, this striving toward the absolute is necessarily implicit in our intellectual acts, and a properly executed transcendental analysis of our powers of cognition will render it explicit.

Second, we must be careful to distinguish between the "content" of thought and the "activity" of thinking by which this content is attained. The content of our thought—what we can conceptually represent—is always finite because of the intellect's dependence on the senses as its source of information about reality. Hence, at the level of representable content, what thought achieves is an indefinite increment in the fund of knowledge, but always within the sphere of the finite. If our analysis is restricted to the content of thought, then we might be led to assert that the undeniable restlessness of the human intellect—its impulse to push beyond any realized content—indicates that its motivating drive is toward an *indefinite* accumulation of data, and not, as Maréchal contends, a primal thrust toward the infinite or absolute.

Such an analysis, however, does not pay sufficient heed to the "activity" of thinking by which the content of thought is generated. The active or agent intellect seeks to transcend all the limits it encounters because its range or degree of openness is primordially beyond any limit as such: it is poised toward the infinite. As one of Maréchal's more lucid commentators, Joseph Donceel, puts it: "The passage from finite to infinite is not gradual but immediate. It is not because this or that amount or intensity of knowledge, goodness, truth, beauty, happiness is not sufficient that our mind does not find rest; it is simply because it is finite. The dynamism of the human mind strives for all-out infinity." [47]

In sum, if we reflect on the activity of thinking, we will realize that it is driven by a primal yearning or pure desire to know. Reflection also reveals that, no matter how vast or complex the fund of knowledge, the intellect will nonetheless experience it as limited so long as it remains within the confines of the finite and contingent. As a result, the originating impetus, giving rise to our intellectual activity, is not to be explained as a mere striving for an indefinite accretion of finite data, but as a pervasive longing to transcend the realm of the finite as such. As Maréchal asserts: "Since the formal object of a tendency is the measure of the amplitude of the end whither this tendency keeps striving, we know that the ultimate satiating end of the intellect must be a reality possessing no limiting determinism, that is, a transcendent object, a subsisting infinite."[48]

Although he holds that only an intuitive grasp of God or the infinite can satisfy our intellectual longing, Maréchal follows Aquinas in proclaiming that the attainment of this end exceeds our unaided finite capacities. This is certainly the case for the human intellect in its embodied state, for its knowledge is discursive or abstractive in nature. To be sure, Aquinas teaches that in this life we can know that God exists, and we can speak of God indirectly, yet intelligibly, by means of analogy; but this in no sense constitutes that saturating intuitive vision of the absolute that would alone quench our intellectual yearning. Aquinas also teaches that even disembodied intellectual substances, despite their intuitive mode of cognition, cannot fulfill their desire for the beatific vision of God (*visio Dei beatifica*) by their own powers. Thus, for Aquinas, the ultimate end of all intellectual striving—what we implicitly seek in all our cognitive operations—can only be ours through an act of grace from God, himself.

> Now, seeing God's substance transcends the limitations of every created nature; indeed, it is proper for each created intellectual nature to understand according to the manner of its own substance. But divine substance cannot be understood in this way. . . . Therefore the attainment by a created intellect to the vision of divine substance is not possible except through the action of God, who transcends all creatures.[49]

But if this is the case, if the achievement of our ultimate intellectual end is beyond our native capacities, how are we to be sure that it is a real possibility for us, and not just a chimera? Certainly not just because we desire it; for, as Maréchal is quick to say, "the fact that we desire an end is not an evident sign of its real possibility."[50] Nor can we, in a rational critique, point to scriptural promises that God will grant us the union with him that we seek.[51] Are we not once again in the throes of the Kantian dilemma?

It should be remembered that Kant affirms that the intellect incessantly seeks to unify experience in ever more comprehensive frameworks, and that the quest for the unconditioned ground of experience inspires this process.[52] This aspect of our rational life naturally gives rise to the idea of God as the infinite and absolute ground of the finite and contingent universe that we encounter. However, according to Kant, we can have no conceptual knowledge of God because the categories of the understanding apply only to sense experience, and cannot be extended beyond that domain without engendering a host of antinomies and confusions. Furthermore, we do not possess a superior intellectual capacity whereby we could intuit God directly without dependence on the sense faculties. From the point of view of pure or theoretical reason, then, God remains the unknown and unknowable.[53]

But the "God hypothesis" is not thereby rendered useless. It serves the vital "regulative" function of driving the understanding beyond any limited synthesis it has attained in search of broader unifications of our experience. For Kant, however, this synthesizing activity is confined to the empirical realm of sense experience and cannot arrive at the transempirical reality of God.[54]

Thus, Kant's analysis holds that the "idea" of God, the unconditioned ground of all experience, plays a vital regulative role in the ongoing process of cognition, but whether there is a reality corresponding to this idea remains undetermined from the point of view of pure or theoretical reason. Certainly, Kant wants to claim that the existence of God is at least a genuine theoretical possibility. His intention in the *Critique of Pure Reason* is to show that the attempt, on theoretical grounds, to move from the "possibility" to the "actuality" of God's existence is illegitimate; that theoretical reason can neither prove nor disprove the existence of God. The God hypothesis thus remains an open possibility, which must be verified on other grounds. Kant endeavors to provide just such a verification on the basis of our moral experience in the *Critique of Practical Reason.*

For Maréchal, reflection discovers the primal drive of the intellect toward the absolute, and this discovery points to the possible existence of God and to a union with him that would quench our intellectual longing.[55] Maréchal moves beyond Kant by demonstrating that, in the case of the absolute being, the possibility of its existence theoretically entails the actuality of its existence.

The Actuality of God

Discursive human consciousness requires the subject-object duality. When we know something, it is immanent in the mind as a content of consciousness. But it can only attain this status if it appears as a known object over against a knowing subject. Even our reflection on our own mental operations requires a distinction between these operations as "known" (object) and the same operations as "knowing" (subject).

Our capacity to distinguish the knower from the known enables us to "objectify" our experience; without it, we would be totally immersed in our environment. Like animals, we would have an awareness of the existence of other things through the senses, but would be unable to classify them as objects of a particular kind. When we consider this fundamental difference between humans and animals, we can see that our dependence on the senses as the source of information about the outside world is not sufficient to explain the vital subject-object duality with which we intellectually encounter reality. Animals are as dependent on sense information as we are, but they do not, strictly speaking, "objectify" their experience. Their knowing differs from human knowing not simply in degree, but in kind.[56]

Our intellectual grasp of reality cannot be explained on the "passive" empiricist model of mind as tabula rasa. If we are to account for the distinctive character of human consciousness, in which we (a) recognize the "other" as "not-I"; (b) classify it as an object of a certain kind; and (c) come to know more and more about its specific nature and its relations to other objects, we most posit some necessary mental activity, which works in concert with the sense faculties.

But if the mind does not passively receive information about external objects, neither does it create this information ex nihilo. In the Thomistic view, the mind intellectually assimilates the forms, abstracted from objects presented to it via sensation, as a partial fulfillment of its quest for knowledge of absolute being. Consequently, the knower (subject) is distinguished from the known (object), as an activity or striving is distinguished from its goal or end. Maréchal explains: "In a discursive intelligence, the assimilated form is opposed to the subject and acquires an 'in itself' insofar as it constitutes, for the subject, a dynamic value, a moment of an active becoming."[57]

Kant saw that the transcendental unity of apperception is a necessary a priori condition for human consciousness. We cannot account for the content of consciousness unless it can be related to an "I" which actually possesses it, and from which it can be formally distinguished. But Kant failed to explicate fully the nature of the "I" (subject) as a continuous activity whose goal is the assimilation of all that is "not-I." Thus, the subject reaches out to the "other," and experiences it precisely as "other" (object), because of the fundamental dynamism that constitutes its nature. As a result, we must not only posit the bare and formal "I think" (transcendental unity of apperception), but also its basic dynamism toward the absolute, as necessary a priori conditions for the possibility of the content of consciousness we actually possess.

Maréchal is well aware that thus far in his transcendental analysis of cognition he has only demonstrated the *psychological* necessity of positing the fundamental dynamism of the intellect toward the absolute. We should add that Kant, himself, gives evidence of realizing this necessity by assigning an indispensable "regulative" function to the "idea" of God or transcendental ideal in the cognitive process. But Maréchal wishes to complete Kant's transcendental turn by showing that this psychological necessity entails a *logical* necessity as well. Maréchal is fully aware that

> from a strictly critical point of view, a dynamic exigency, however ineluctable, establishes only, by itself alone, a subjective certitude. Therefore we must still show that the "reality in themselves" of these ends, which are necessarily intended in the very exercise of every discursive thought, is for the knowing subject not only a dynamic exigency but a logical necessity.[58]

To achieve this end, Maréchal focuses on the fundamental encounter between the natural dynamism of the intellect and the requisite empirical content provided by the senses. As noted earlier, this content is assimilated by the intellect as a moment or stage in its ultimate quest for absolute being. The intellect abstracts the forms of sensible objects as "subordinate" ends relative to its "final" end, namely, assimilation with absolute being.

> Hence the native dynamism of the intellect grasps the empirical determinations as a beginning or participation of this end, and the dim volition by which it assimilates them is but the very volition of this end itself. Thus the "empirical determination" of the first intellectual act enters into the mind's dynamism not only as assimilated to the natural form, but also as referred to the proper end of this dynamism.[59]

Now, it would be contradictory and altogether absurd to strive for an end that one knows to be completely impossible and unattainable. If the end in question is a finite, contingent object, the mere possibility of eventually attaining it is sufficient warrant to render one's efforts toward it rational and coherent. Even if a particular finite object does not currently exist, one might still sensibly strive for it, provided that there is some possibility of its existing at the completion of one's efforts.

If, however, the end in question is infinite, absolute, and necessary, the situation is radically altered. Maréchal explains that

> when this object is God, when the objective end is identified with the Being which is necessary by itself (Pure Act) which has no other mode of reality than absolute existence, the dialectical exigency implied by the desire assumes a new scope, not merely on account of the natural desire, but on account of the nature of the desire's object. To affirm of God that he is possible is the same as to affirm that he exists, since his existence is the condition of every possibility.[60]

The logic of Maréchal's argument to this point can be summarized as follows: (*a*) transcendental analysis shows that a finalistic dynamism underlies all our cognitive operations; (*b*) since no conceivable finite or contingent achievement could possibly satisfy this dynamism, its ultimate end must be the absolute, necessary being or God; (c) thus, our striving for this being qualifies as a necessary a priori condition for the possibility of cognition as such, and every intellectual act by which we comprehend some finite entity must be seen as a subordinate movement toward absolute being; (d) the fundamental striving toward God, which is a necessary precondition for cognition as such, implies that God is possible; (e) in the case of God alone—the necessary being whose existence grounds the possibility for the contingent existence of everything else that "is"—possible existence entails actual existence. Accordingly, Maréchal concludes that "we may state in strictest logic, that the possibility of our subjective last end presupposes logically the existence of our objective last end, God. Thus, in every intellectual act, we affirm *implicitly* the existence of an absolute Being."[61]

It is not that we can conceptually capture the essence of God as part of our content of consciousness. As infinite being, God transcends the limited categories by which we catalogue and comprehend the finite realities of our experience. Furthermore, as Maréchal makes repeatedly clear, we cannot bypass the limitations of discursive reasoning and catch a glimpse of the essence of God by a foray of intuitive insight. In fact, when we seek to understand the finite entities that surround us, we are not even immediately aware of God, in an explicit fashion, as the ultimate end of our intellectual striving.[62] Indeed, we can spend a lifetime trying to understand the myriad finite objects that enter our experience without ever seriously scrutinizing the very activity by which such "understanding" comes about. Even a thinker as perspicacious as Kant stopped short of a thorough explication of those conditions implicit in the dynamic operation of cognition. Kant correctly depicted this process as a synthesis of sense and intellect, but he failed to investigate fully the primal driving force undergirding all cognitive striving, namely, the human quest for the infinite, unconditioned, necessary ground of all that exists. And, argues Maréchal, it was this failure to pursue his transcendental analysis to the very core of the cognitive process that gave rise to Kant's agnostic posture vis-à-vis God from the point of theoretical reason; and that moved Kant to relegate the "idea" of God to a "regulative," rather than a "constitutive," role in cognition.

Beyond Kant

The unfinished character of Kant's transcendental analysis also leads to his bifurcation of reality into phenomena and noumena. For Kant, our knowledge of phenomena (reality as synthesized by the a priori structures of the mind) entails the existence of noumena (that same reality as it is in itself, independent of the mind's synthesizing activity). Maréchal believes that Kant was correct in affirming the logical necessity of the noumenon or thing-in-itself (*Ding an sich*), but he argues that Kant neglected to unearth completely the grounds for such an affirmation.

> Kant defines the thing-in-itself as an absolute reality which limits the phenomena. Now in order to know a limit as limit one must, if deprived of the immediate intuition of the domain extending beyond this limit, encounter this side of it a dynamic principle which virtually surmounts it. The Kantian reasoning would have made its point on one condition: that the phenomenon should reveal its own limitation by standing in the way of an objectivating impulse striving beyond it; in brief by opposing itself to a tendency which would carry the subject through the phenomena towards an ulterior term which is no longer phenomenal.[63]

Kant was barred from this insight because he construed our mental representations in a static manner as the object (*id quod*) of knowledge, rather than the means (*id quo*) by which the dynamic process of cognition attains to knowledge. When we understand our mental life in this fashion, we will search in vain for a bridge between the interior recesses of thought and the exterior realm of being.

However, as Maréchal has shown, the human mind is, at root, a continual striving toward absolute being, and all our mental operations are moments in this ongoing process. Our concepts are not isolated from being or turned in on themselves; rather, they serve as the vehicles by which we plumb the depths of the reality we encounter in search, finally, of its ultimate foundation. In other words, what we come to "know" in the first instance are individual beings against the background of our striving for absolute being, not the mental operations by which we achieve such knowledge. Of course, we can formally reflect on these operations in order to dissect and analyze their constituent elements, but if we mistakenly treat them as ends in themselves, isolating them from their instrumental role in cognition, what emerges is a fabricated dichotomy between thought and being.

We are primordially and undeniably "beings-in-the-world." Descartes's *res cogitans*, isolated and secure in its own subjectivity, is thus a mental fiction; for there can be no subjectivity without the objectivity of the world standing inexorably over against it. Our judgments (affirmative and negative) are not about our mental operations as such, but about the things we are struggling to know *through* these operations. From this vantage point, the notion that we are entrapped in a mental or ideal realm, and require a bridge to the realm of things-in-themselves, takes on the appearance of a pseudoproblem, which flies in the face of our daily dealings with the world. Our epistemological ruminations ought to represent our genuine lived experience, and not take their point of departure from an artificially constructed locus.

For Maréchal, the ontological critique of Aristotelian-Thomistic realism reflects this natural tendency of the mind: "The ontological critique of the ancients starts from the 'objects' considered in the fullness of their objectivity, that is, posited absolutely, as eventual ends (things)."[64] The ontological critique endeavors to explicate and justify theoretically our natural tendency—born of our daily contact with the world—to affirm a primal harmony between thought and being which is encapsulated in the "correspondence theory of truth" (*adaequatio intellectus et rei*). Through his historical analysis, Maréchal has shown how Aristotle defended the harmonious relationship between thought and being against the theoretical attacks of the Sophists. Aristotle demonstrated that in the "act" of denying truth the Sophists ineluctably affirm its existence. Aquinas retrieved this Aristotelian epistemological perspective for the Middle Ages, but his efforts were undermined by the impact of late medieval nominalism. In time this launched a renewed questioning of the theoretical warrant for our "practical" acceptance of the natural correspondence between thought and being. What resulted were the many failed attempts by rationalists and empiricists to give a philosophically adequate account of cognition.

In response to Hume's skepticism, Kant inaugurated his Copernican revolution in philosophy by employing the method of transcendental analysis. It is Maréchal's primary contention that a rigorously pursued transcendental analysis of the generation of the immanent objects of consciousness (mental representations or concepts) reveals their *instrumental* role in the overarching, dynamic process of cognition, whose ultimate end is assimilation with absolute being. Maréchal explains:

> Considering . . . the successive acts of the intellect, reflection discovers in them, through an authentic inner experimentation, the correlation of a basic dynamism which is at work everywhere and of an ultimate subjective end which is always intended. Now unless one be willing to deny being and to adopt contradiction, the admission of a necessarily intended ultimate subjective end entails the affirmation of a necessarily existing objective end. Thus we not only know implicitly but we discover clearly and explicitly, in the *a priori* conditions of our primitive perceptions of objects, the at first latent revelation of the absolute Being as universal End.[65]

Basic to Maréchal's effort to rejuvenate metaphysical analysis is his continual call for a holistic approach to cognition: one that does not disengage any of its constituent elements from their complementary roles in the total process. In his historical propaedeutic, Maréchal recounts how epistemological theories that sever the functioning of the senses from that of the intellect generate a one-sided empiricism; conversely, those that sever the functioning of the intellect from that of the senses generate a dogmatic rationalism. These truncated accounts of cognition give rise to insoluble dilemmas and thus represent philosophical positions crippled from the outset by fragmentary points of departure.

In his treatment of Kant, Maréchal wishes to illustrate that the categorial or conceptualizing function of the mind cannot be detached from its primal quest for the absolute. In other words, an a priori commitment to the intelligibility of the universe, and to our ability to fathom its structures, underlies *all* our intellectual operations. Even the strict skeptic must at least assume the intelligible coherence of the claims he makes about the nature of things; otherwise he would not bother to speak and, if consistent, should reduce himself to a state of silent, thoughtless stupor.

From Maréchal's perspective, the very possibility of thought entails an adherence to the principle of intelligibility or sufficient reason, which affirms that everything that "is" has a sufficient reason for its existence—or that which is not intelligible in itself is intelligible only by being related to that which is intelligible in itself. Furthermore, the dynamism of the intellect is rooted in the continual quest for the independently intelligible core of the universe that this principle demands. We experience the "finite" character of the things we encounter precisely because we are aware that they are not intelligible in themselves; thus, they fall short of the ultimate end of our intellectual striving. Hence, the intelligibility of the universe is dependent on the existence of an absolute being, which is intelligible in itself, and which consequently serves as the ultimate source or ground of the intelligibility of the finite beings of our experience. Expressed in another fashion, the contingent beings that we know are only relatively intelligible in that their existence (*esse*) is not self-explanatory, but must be referred to something else. Their "finiteness" consists primordially in a limitation of being. As a result, the intellect's demand for complete intelligibility can only be met if, and only if, it can discover a self-explanatory being whose necessary existence can prove a sufficient reason for the existence of contingent being.

Maréchal does not rest content with simply demonstrating the subjective utility of a commitment to the "possible" existence of a necessary being as the end (*terminus ad quem*) of intellectual striving. If the ultimate end of cognition is merely possible, then the objectivity of knowledge, and the attainment of truth as a correspondence between thought and being, is only probable at best. Maréchal wants to set the human cognitive quest on a certain foundation, namely, that of knowing that its ultimate object, the absolute being, exists not only in thought but in actuality as well. If such a foundation is assured, then the search for total intelligibility is neither illusory nor capricious. Though we grope and struggle to make sense out of reality, which may often be resistant to our persistent probings, we can nonetheless be confident that we are not adrift in an

absurd, unintelligible flux, whose sheer relativity and conting-
ence ultimately defy rational scrutiny.

Maréchal, the Ontological Argument, and the Quest for the Absolute

One might readily agree that Maréchal has convincingly revealed the a priori commitment to the principle of sufficient
reason undergirding all our cognitive operations. But has he
shown that this commitment represents any more than a heuristic assumption by which we make our way in the world?

To address this decisive question properly, let us examine
Maréchal's move from the "subjective" to the "objective"
necessity of positing the existence of an absolute being in
terms of the age-old controversy surrounding the ontological
argument. Maréchal is attempting to anchor the necessary affirmation of the "possibility" of God's existence in an incontro-
vertible aspect of our experience; namely, in the mind's natural
thrust toward the absolute, and not merely in a formal idea of
the absolute considered solely in itself. In so doing, he hopes to
circumvent the standard objection to the ontological argument
that it involves an unwarranted leap from the ideal to the real
order. The classical argument starts with a concept; thus, it can
only end with a concept, not with the necessary affirmation of
an actually existing being. What Anselm demonstrates is that
God, as the greatest conceivable being (*id quo majus cogitari
non potest*), must be *thought* of as existing in reality, not that
this God *actually* exists. The "idea" of God entails the "idea"
of necessary existence, but the actual existence of God cannot
be demonstrated by virtue of logical or conceptual analysis
alone. Donceel explains the thrust of Maréchal's argument
well when he writes:

> An examination of the movement of our intellect has shown us
> that our intellect implicitly affirms the possibility of God every
> time it affirms something. Thus the possibility of God is not arrived
> at by a mere examination of concepts but is implied as an undeni-
> able fact of everybody's experience, the dynamism of the intellect.[66]

At this juncture, one might be persuaded that our infinite
cognitive striving implicitly demands the positive possibility of

God's actual existence. But one might still object that striving for something does not imply that it really exists. If something really exists, it must be possible; but possibility alone does not imply real existence. Maréchal contends that the preceding statement is always true *except* in the case of the absolute being, whose definitive characteristic is "necessary existence." Unlike finite (contingent) realities, if the absolute being does not exist, it is not possible. Stated positively, the absolute being is possible if, and only if, it exists. Hence, for this being, and this being alone, possibility implies actual existence.

In Maréchal's argument, God is treated as an a priori condition we posit to account for our striving for the infinite or absolute. It must be remembered that the method of transcendental analysis begins with an undeniable fact of experience (our content of consciousness) and then proceeds to uncover the conditions for its possibility. An affirmation of the former entails a necessary affirmation of the latter. The ontological argument provides us with, what we might call, the logic of "God": it explicates what we mean when we use the term, but on its own it does not prove that this term has an objective reference in our experience. Maréchal has employed transcendental analysis to locate an indirect but nonetheless actually existing and necessary reference to God as the ultimate end or goal of the intellectual dynamism at the heart of the cognitive process. This reference is not merely "regulative" but "constitutive" of the content of consciousness we actually possess. As Donceel nicely puts it:

> How can we ever hope to bridge the infinite gap between God and the things of experience? The fact is that we do not have to bridge it; we do not really arrive at God. We start with him; we are with him from the beginning. He is already in our mind when we know our first object, when we make our first affirmation, since only he makes them possible for us. We reach God at once or never at all all. . . . Augustine and Pascal have grasped this basic way in which our mind knows God when they present him as telling us: "You would not be looking for me if you had not already found me."[67]

Maréchal believes that he has shown that our thought and the quest for intelligible order are indissolubly linked; the principle of intelligibility or sufficient reason holds sway over all our intellectual operations. Such a principle cannot be demonstrated, for we would necessarily employ it and assume its validity in the very attempt at demonstration. Even the most radical skeptic, in his efforts to gainsay this principle, implicitly and necessarily makes use of it. Hence, an a priori commitment to the validity of the principle of intelligibility is a necessary condition for the very activity of thinking.

Such a commitment is implicit in the following statement by Stephen Toulmin: "The mainspring of science is the conviction that by honest, imaginative enquiry we can build up a system of ideas about nature which has some legitimate claim to reality."[68] The qualifying phrase, "some legitimate claim," functions here as a caveat against an uncritical acceptance of *any* "system of ideas"; but it does not imply that the search for intelligibility may be utterly in vain on the chance that there is no intelligible order to be discovered. Seen in this light, contemporary relativists or deconstructionists are certainly justified in attacking dogmatic claims to absolute truth wherever they find them. However, in the midst of the intellectual fray which marks the search for truth, Maréchal's analysis is an instructive reminder that the principle of intelligibility cannot be surrendered without undermining the very possibility of coherent thought.

Maréchal further contends that our necessary commitment to this principle entails an implicit affirmation of the existence of God, the absolute being. It is because of this implicit affirmation that we recognize the entities we encounter as "finite," and then seek to render them intelligible through ever-broadening analysis.

> The representations which are immanent to our thought possess in it the value of objects only in virtue of an implicit affirmation; not of any affirmation, however, but in virtue of a metaphysical affirmation which connects the object with the absolute realm of being. Hence the metaphysical affirmation, as a dynamic attitude, is really the condition of the possibility of the object in our mind, that is, in a discursive mind.[69]

The necessary affirmation of God implicit in cognition does not require, as a correlate, that we can adequately represent God through concepts. Nonetheless, we can affirm, mean, or intend more than we can picture conceptually. In this context, Karl Rahner asserts that God is never an object of knowledge that can be represented, but the "whither" (*worauf*) of all intellectual striving. Echoing Maréchal, he speaks of a nonconceptual pre-apprehension (*Vorgriff*) of absolute being as a necessary condition of the possibility of cognition. Then he cautions:

> This is in no sense an *"a priori"* proof of God's existence. For the pre-apprehension and its "whither" can be proven and affirmed as present and necessary for all knowledge only in the *a posteriori* apprehension of a real existent and as the necessary condition of the latter. The proofs of God's existence in Thomas are only the application of this situation in his metaphysics of knowledge to his ontology of the real. The real and limited existent that is affirmed requires as its condition the reality of an unlimitable absolute *esse*. Instead of this we have simply said: the affirmation of the real limitation of an existent has as its condition the pre-apprehension of *esse*, which implicitly and simultaneously affirms an absolute *esse*.[70]

In sum, when cognition is viewed holistically, we see that our primal intellectual orientation toward absolute being gives rise to and dominates the process by which we come to know finite things. Through our pre-apprehension that their being does not embody the unlimited being toward which we are tending, we recognize these things as finite and transform them into objects of our knowledge; they represent an analogous and partial expression of that fullness of being which alone can satiate our pure desire to know. For Maréchal, then, an explicit recognition and appreciation of the fundamental dynamism toward the absolute at the core of all intellectual operations is the genuine *point de départ de la métaphysique.*

> The absolute has placed its mark on the fundamental tendency of our intelligence, such that this tendency constantly transcends particular intellections: the mind, through its internal dynamism, is driven from intellection to intellection, from object to object, but as long as it remains in the realm of the finite, it strives in vain to equal its own internal movement. . . . And this unevenness . . . is the very condition of reasoning, the catalyst of that always

dissatisfied curiosity in which the scholastics of old rightly discovered the principle of all speculation. Thus the human mind is a faculty in search of its intuition [*une faculté en quête de son intuition*], that is, of assimilation with being, with pure and simple being, supremely one, without restriction, without distinction as to essence and existence or possibility or actuality.[71]

CHAPTER FIVE

Critique and Conclusion

Conservative Thomist Critique

As we have seen, Maréchal attempted to effect a rapprochement between the "realism" of the Aristotelian-Thomistic tradition and the demands of "critical philosophy" based on transcendental analysis. Some more traditional Thomists, most notably Etienne Gilson, have questioned the very possibility of such a reconciliation. Of Maréchal's enterprise Gilson writes:

> The whole question here is whether it is possible to overcome Kantian agnosticism "starting from its own principles." To this we must answer: no, for Kantian agnosticism is inscribed within the principles from which it flows, which is precisely why they are principles. Therefore, if you engage in a critique that in no way prejudges its object you may be able to extricate yourself from Kantian agnosticism, but you will not have done so by starting with its own principles. It will be necessary to make a fresh start. If, however, you do indeed start from the principles of Kantian agnosticism, you will necessarily fall prey to the very agnosticism you were seeking to avoid.[1]

Gilson is arguing that realism cannot be vindicated by a method that takes the "immanent object" or "content of consciousness" as its point of departure. If one starts by isolating the thinking subject within the realm of its own subjectivity—cut off from the objective reality that stands inexorably over against it—one will look in vain for a way to rejoin that reality, and thus some variant of idealism must be the inevitable outcome.

As the first four volumes of *Le Point de Départ* make abundantly clear, Maréchal was acutely aware how faulty and fragmented points of departure had vitiated the efforts of even the most gifted and well-intentioned philosophers in the Western tradition. His hope was that his work in historical analysis and critique would shed light on the vagaries of Western thought since the emergence of late medieval nominalism, and demonstrate that only a metaphysical vision akin to the critical realism of the Aristotelian-Thomistic tradition could give an adequate account of the cognitive process.

Viewed against the historical background of continental rationalism and Humean skepticism, Kant's transcendental method can be seen as a partial reappropriation of the insights of ancient and medieval Aristotelian realism, in that Kant rediscovered the necessity of postulating a complementary relation of sense and understanding in the acquisition of knowledge. Although post-Kantian idealists recaptured the dynamic character of intellectual striving lost to Kant's overly static conception of the understanding (*Verstand*), Kant and his idealist successors still labored under the baneful influence of the defective assumptions that had afflicted Western philosophy in the preceding centuries. So, as Otto Muck tell us:

> Within the historical perspective, it is understandable why Kant sees the transcendental method as anti-metaphysical and why Kant's successors were able to develop the method further without arriving at a realistic metaphysics. Historically, it is entirely possible to separate the basic structure of the transcendental method from particular instances of its special adaption. It is then possible to ask whether or not this method is capable of correcting erroneous views which crop up in some of the concrete expressions of the transcendental method. This is exactly what Maréchal attempts to do with respect to the anti-metaphysical and idealist views which have been connected with the method in relation to Kant and German Idealism.[2]

Specifically, Maréchal strives to demonstrate that a rigorous application of the transcendental method, unfettered by the faulty presuppositions of Kant and his immediate successors, can begin with the immanent object of consciousness and, in seeking the conditions for its possibility, arrive at the necessity of relating that immanent object to the real order of being, thereby providing a transcendental deduction of objective affirmation. In a reply to Jacques Maritain, in which he endeavors to justify his methodology, Maréchal asks why he should not

> begin with the phenomenal object, from a methodological point of view (*ad modum quaestionis solvendae*) and polemically (*elenchice*) as something given, since this is admitted by those who reject every mode of determinate metaphysics, and then attempt to show that a purely phenomenal object cannot be an object (in consciousness). . . . This is the leitmotif of my fifth volume.[3]

Maréchal does not for a moment doubt the validity of the objective affirmation of being that is the hallmark of ancient and medieval realism. However, he tries to show with painstaking precision just why such an affirmation has been called into question in modern philosophy. In addition, Maréchal attempts to meet Kant and his successors within their own arena and show that, even starting with what they considered indubitable (namely, our content of consciousness) and proceeding to employ their method, one must in the end recognize the necessity of objective affirmation. In this sense, Maréchal must be distinguished from those more conservative Thomists who, eschewing even the possibility of fruitful dialogue with the various strains of idealism, merely rest their case for realism on the "self-evident" fact that in our knowledge we grasp real being.[4] Once again, as Otto Muck points out:

> Maréchal's approach to the theory of knowledge is distinguished from others in that he does not simply accept the legitimacy of the claim of knowledge to grasp real being through a mere appeal to what is evident, but derives the validity of this evidence from the conditions of possibility of the act of knowledge.[5]

Although, like Gilson and other Thomists, Maréchal was fully cognizant of the maladies of modern philosophy, he did not consider the intellectual condition of his Kantian and idealist adversaries to be irremediable. Nor did he feel bound to accept Kant's principles and conclusions in their entirety, since he believed that he had shown through historical and critical analysis that they were beset with certain limitations and inconsistencies. The essence of Maréchal's project was to demonstrate that, with some warranted adjustments, the transcendental method need not necessarily lead to Kant's negative conclusions about metaphysics, nor to the absolute idealism of Kant's successors.[6]

The Charge of Ontologism

Maréchal's transcendental Thomism has also been negatively characterized as a brand of ontologism. Consider the following remarks by R. Heinz:

> If the absolute Being of God is necessarily the precondition and goal of finite knowing, of objectivation, then the objectivation that is only achieved by means of the precondition and by means of this goal is the direct knowledge of God, even if it is merely in a discursive, finite fashion. The object that would result from this objectifying process at any given moment would be a mode of God (*Modus Gottes*)—the totality of objects involved in a system, supposing such a system is possible, would be God himself.[7]

I have noted a number of times in the course of this study that Maréchal rejects all forms of ontologism which presuppose an intuitive capacity for insight into reality that bypasses the contributions of the senses.[8] Along with Aristotle and Aquinas, Maréchal is committed to a discursive model of the intellect that is always related to sense experience. He further holds that our ability to conceptualize reality is grounded in an intellectual dynamism whose ultimate end is the absolute, and that the existence of this absolute is a necessary precondition of all acts of knowledge.

> If the final end of our intellect is the absolute Being, our initial intellectual power is unlimited in the order of intelligibles; and the final object of our intelligence, far from being representable by whatever diversity of characters, only reveals itself indirectly, in the

infinite perspective of the tendency [*tendance*]; not as a definable form, but as the "beyond" [*au delà*] of all forms absolutely.⁹

Maréchal goes to great lengths to unmask the inadequacies of the various manifestations of ontologism in the history of Western philosophy. Thus, to accuse him of falling prey to ontologist assumptions bespeaks a basic misunderstanding of his work. In this regard, I am in full agreement with Harold Holz when he states that an ontologist or direct access to the absolute "contradicts the fundamental intentions, the entire project as well as a wealth of contrary statements on the part of Maréchal. In addition, there is not a single member of his school who explicitly or implicitly would give occasion for such a conclusion." ¹⁰

Maréchal and Hegel

Maréchal contends that, in Hegel's thought,

> the world, objective creation, becomes . . . a necessary moment in the internal evolving cycle of God. . . . By means of a verbal fiction God and the world, the absolute and the relative, are still opposed, but, when all is said and done, there is only one God, only one Absolute—the totality. To confuse the totality with the absolute is clearly what characterizes pantheism. Every philosophic conception which eliminates the contingency of creation leads inevitably to this.¹¹

Quentin Lauer counters that, in his own lifetime, Hegel defended himself against just such a charge. Hegel argued strenuously that he in no sense wished simply to identify God with the totality of finite reality. In fact, one of his major critical aims was to expose the inadequacy of thinking of the "infinite" in mathematical guise as the endless extension of the finite.

For Hegel, and for Maréchal as well, the infinite or absolute is the necessary being (*causa sui*) that is the ground of finite or contingent being. Hegel envisions his task as an explication, in speculative (*vernunftig*) terms, of a basic Christian theological perspective, namely, that God, the almighty creator of the universe, is likewise an omnipresent, providential force within this creation. Lauer notes that "Hegel never speaks of reason *discovering* the reality of God, but only of "speculative thinking" *seeing* the rationality of the God of faith."[12]

In this sense, Hegel considered himself a continuator of the Anselmian project, "faith seeking understanding" (*fides quaerens intellectum*). This led him, in his own historical situation, to oppose those who saw a discontinuity between faith and reason (theology and philosophy), such as Kant, Jacobi, and Schleiermacher. One of the major goals of Hegel's philosophizing was to show the rationality of Christian theism which is grounded in the assumption that the finite and the infinite are continuous yet distinguishable. After all, according to Christian theology, God did create the universe ex nihilo and it is utterly dependent on his almighty power (continuity or immanence), but the universe cannot, on that account, simply be identified with God (distinction or transcendence). Hegel's approach was to attempt to overcome the apparent contradiction between the finite and the infinite by conceiving God as the "concrete universal" that particularizes itself in finite manifestations, without surrendering its own infinite universality. As Lauer puts it:

> In his *Lectures on the History of Philosophy* Hegel seeks to resolve the contradiction by appealing to what is a constant in his thought, to the concept of God as *the* concretely universal, that is, universal by embracing, not by eliminating, all differentiation. "The concrete . . . is the universal which particularizes itself and in this particularization, finitization, still remains in itself infinite." It is characteristic of the authentically infinite that in "othering" itself it does not cease to be itself, that is does not cease to be infinite.[13]

I believe that Lauer's criticism of Maréchal on this score is well taken. For all his perspicacity, thoroughness, and boldness in dealing with Kant, Maréchal does not seem to have risen above the standard polemical treatment of Hegel that was common fare in neo-Thomist circles in order to penetrate to a deeper understanding of the Hegelian corpus. One need not find all of Hegel's philosophical peregrinations enlightening, nor be quite as sanguine as Lauer about the compatibility of Hegelian philosophy and the tenets of Christian theology, to see that Maréchal's dismissal of the rich insights that Hegel does offer on the stock charge of "pantheism" is unwarranted.

In fact, I would argue that there is much to be gained from a comparative analysis of Transcendental Thomism and Hegel's philosophy. Most importantly, both Maréchal and Hegel stress the linkage between the intelligibility of the universe and the affirmation of the existence of God. Both deny that the finite as finite can be adequately understood: as a contingent reality, the finite is only intelligible against the background of that which is noncontingent or necessary. In other words, the intelligibility of the finite being of the universe depends, in the form of a transcendental precondition, on the existence of God, the necessary being. As Hegel expresses it: "Not because the contingent is but, on the contrary, because it is non-Being, merely phenomenal, because its Being is not true reality, the absolute necessity is. This latter is its Being and Truth."[14]

Hence, Maréchal and Hegel jointly hold that the necessary affirmation of God's existence is revealed when we properly attend to the "activity" of thinking, to that quest for total intelligibility that is the quintessential feature of *Homo sapiens*. The desire to know, which underlies and motivates our cognitive activity, is grounded in the assumption that the "real" is "rational," or that being is intelligible. But both Maréchal and Hegel argue that the rationality or intelligibility of the universe is ultimately dependent on the existence of God, the necessary being. Consequently, the validity of our drive to understand all that we confront is indissolubly linked to God as a fundamental precondition. When we view the cognitive process in accordance with Maréchal's and Hegel's doctrines, we can truly say that only if God "is," can we be said to understand anything at all. Lauer explains:

> To speak . . . of "proofs" (or of a "proof") for the existence of God is not to speak of a way of arriving at God by beginning with what is not God. It is the recognition that God is present from the beginning in all true thought, in all true knowledge. But because this very recognition requires the labor of speculative thinking, it can be said that God is "proved" if thinking is recognized for what it is. Thinking is the ineluctable logical march of the concept to objectivity, and the ultimate objectivity short of which thought cannot stop (and still be thought) is the reality of God.[15]

In sum, I would maintain that there are good grounds for arguing that the posture of Transcendental Thomism vis-à-vis

Hegelian philosophy ought to be one of critical correlation, rather than suspicion or out-and-out rejection.[16]

"Soft" Justification

It is also important to emphasize that, like Hegel, Maréchal is seeking a "theoretical" and not merely a "practical" (in the Kantian sense) justification for the existence of God as the ultimate guarantor of the intelligibility of the universe and the objectivity of our knowledge. In this respect, his work must be sharply distinguished from that of many contemporary philosophers and theologians who, accepting the legitimacy of the Kantian split between the theoretical and practical capacities of reason, argue that *only* "practical" justifications of the rationality of belief in God are possible. As an example of this line of argument, consider the following remarks of Hans Küng in reference to Kant:

> It is not by a theoretical proof of reason, but only by a practically recognized (but completely rationally justifiable) fundamental trust on the part of the whole person, that I become certain that the self, human freedom and perhaps also God are not merely ideas, but "realities." All these basic questions must be answered not on the basis of pure reason but on that of living and considered practice.[17]

As we have seen, Maréchal is critical of Kant's bifurcation of our intellectual capacities into theoretical and practical reason, and his employment of the latter as the sole pathway to meta-empirical affirmations. Maréchal holds that such "practical" demonstrations—however consoling and useful—nonetheless represent a form of dogmatism or fideism unless the postulates of practical reason can be fortified by the rigor of theoretical justification.[18]

Küng, on the other hand, follows Kant in affirming that theoretical reason leaves the question of the ultimate meaningfulness of reality open and unresolved.[19] He then argues that this stalemate can be broken by our decision to adopt an attitude of "fundamental trust" toward reality (a "yes" to God) that offers a "practical" ground for our moral and intellectual striving.[20]

For John Mackie, one of Küng's critics, there is no practical necessity to postulate God's existence to ground an anti-nihilist commitment.

> Ironically, he [Küng] has himself supplied all the materials for showing that the challenge of both intellectual and moral or practical nihilism can be met on purely human terms, by what Küng calls a "fundamental trust" which is reasonable in its own right— that is equivalently, by a fallibilist empiricism on the intellectual side and on the practical side by the invention of value. The further postulation of a God, even as indeterminate and mysterious a God as Küng's, is a gratuitous addition, an attempted underpinning which is as needless as it is incomprehensible.[21]

As I have stated, Maréchal refuses to accept an unbridgeable gap between theoretical and practical reason. He eschews all "soft" attempts to support metaphysical claims—including the existence of God—that issue from a purported necessity to affirm things as "practical" beings that we cannot justify as "theoretical" beings. Maréchal has attempted to show that our theoretical and practical activities are both rooted in our primal striving toward the infinite or absolute. Thus, to posit a divide between intellect and will, is to introduce an artificial incoherence into our human faculties, which are united in the quest for the same ultimate end.

Maréchal would dispute Küng's admission that nihilism is theoretically irrefutable. Although the enunciation of a nihilist or skeptical posture does not contain a formal-logical contradiction (the statements "existence is meaningless" or "there is no truth" do not entail a logically incoherent use of terms), it nonetheless does contain a "performative" contradiction, in that the "content" of its statements contradicts the very activity by which they are made. More precisely, if Maréchal's transcendental analysis of the cognition is correct, then the intelligibility of the universe cannot be coherently called into question, for the assumption of such intelligibility grounds the very possibility of the questioning process, itself.

Furthermore, in response to Küng's critics, Maréchal would retort that neither the fallibilist empiricist nor the pragmatic moralist gives an adequate account of the activity of cognition. In Maréchal's view, an adequate account of such activity will show it as a moment in our continual striving for the absolute. Hence, the affirmation of the absolute or God is a transcendental precondition for the activity of cognition, as such.

Maréchal and Victor Preller on Aquinas

There is an implicit critique of Maréchal's appropriation of the thought of Aquinas in Victor Preller's celebrated "analytic" interpretation of the Angelic Doctor, *Divine Science and the Science of God*.[22] Preller points out that the "phantasm"—so central to the Aristotelian-Thomistic account of cognition—is an odd entity: it has its origin in the impact of the physical object on the senses, but is, itself, a mental construct, thus providing a "doorway" between the physical (material) and mental (nonmaterial) realms. Although he insists on the mythic character of the phantasm, Preller still asserts:

> The notion of a "phantasm" is a theoretical notion which results from reflection on the completed act of conscious perception; it postulates an isomorphism between the physical state of the sensory system and the external cause of sensation, and it draws attention to the operational unity of sensation and intellection in the act of perception. The notion of a "phantasm" does not refer to an "intentional image" but rather to the entire organic process by means of which we perceive and thus know the objects of sense experience.[23]

Maréchal certainly wishes to avoid a static, literalizing interpretation of scholastic language that would distort Aquinas's intention to present cognition as a dynamic activity of the entire human person, both body and soul. Thus, terms such as "phantasm," "agent intellect," and "possible intellect" should not be reified and construed as distinct entities, but should be seen as theoretical constructs to describe vital moments in one, organically functioning process. As Maréchal plainly states:

> The phantasm's instrumental causality consists merely in providing a specification to the efficiency of the agent intellect. Such a cooperation becomes inconceivable if we think of the cooperating elements as distinct entities. But if we think of them as merely the

partial functions of one simple, radical activity, we see how, through it, the agent intellect imprints upon the possible intellect a formal determination molded after the qualitative features of the phantasm.[24]

Thus, Maréchal and Preller would seem to agree that, when properly interpreted, Aquinas provides us with an epistemological account that rightly stresses the operational unity of sense and intellect and the dynamic character of cognition. But Preller goes on to assert:

> The notion of "intentional stuff" over against the "physical stuff" of bodies is manifestly an analogy and serves only to express the unresolved "mind-body problem," not to solve it. What it really means to say that man is a thinking animal—that he has a mind—is known only to God (and perhaps to the neurophysicist of the future). It follows that we do not *know* precisely what is going on "in the mind"; there may be operations of the "mind" or "soul" of which man, in his linguistic and conceptual self-awareness knows nothing.[25]

In the spirit of Aquinas, Maréchal does not claim to provide an exhaustive or definitive description of mental functioning. What we know of the intellect can only be inferred from its acts; for in our present state we are not privy to a direct intuition into its essence or nature. Thus, Maréchal would be in accord with Preller to the extent that all our epistemological insights are based on a finite, imperfect level of analysis. What Maréchal would insist on, however, is a nonreductionist approach to the dilemma posed by the apparently incommensurable "physical-object language" and "mental-state language" that we must employ to describe different aspects of our cognitive experience.

Such an insistence is particularly vital in our decidedly naturalistic age, with its marked proclivity to banish all explanatory models that posit levels of being which are nonmaterial in nature, and thus not amenable to the objectivist probes of physical science. In this context, Maréchal's appropriation of Thomistic epistemology, with its emphasis on the irreducible complementarity of sense and intellect in the cognitive process, can be seen as a countervailing intellectual challenge to the reductionist spirit that now permeates the social and life sciences, and even philosophy as well. Maréchal's purpose in this regard can be naturally conjoined with that of a thinker like Michael Polanyi, who affirms:

> We start from the fact that no material process governed by the laws of matter as known today can conceivably account for the presence of consciousness in material bodies. I have refused to assume that if we succeeded in revising the laws of physics and chemistry, so as to account for the sentience of animals and man, these would still appear to us as automata—with the super-added absurdity of a totally ineffectual mental life accompanying their automatic performances. To represent living men as insentient is empirically false, but to regard them as thoughtful automata is logical nonsense.[26]

The point to stress is that the "activity" by which we come to know cannot be reduced to a mélange of highly complex material (physical) interactions. It requires that we posit a metaphysical level of being—operating in constant conjunction with our physical, organic processes—which our mental or intentional language analogically seeks to depict.

Another area that Preller subjects to scrutiny is Aquinas's doctrine that being is the primal object of the intellect:

> To have the concept of "existence" or "being" is to be naturally disposed to use one's conceptual system to refer to the objects of experience. The concept "being" is not an element in a conceptual system, but a dispositional tendency to compose or bring together the formal intelligibility of a conceptual system and the contents of sense experience in order to use the resultant forms to refer to that which is not immanent in human consciousness. . . . In that sense, "existence" or "being" is the "first concept of the intellect"—the primal concept.[27]

Preller takes this "dispositional tendency" to employ a conceptual system to inform our sense experience as an undeniable given of our intellectual life—a necessary precondition of intellectual consciousness—but he seeks no justification or grounding for this tendency other than its pragmatic necessity.

For Maréchal, it is precisely this tendency of the intellect to render our sense experience ever more intelligible that stands in most urgent need of further explication if we are ever to give an adequate account of cognition. The divergence between Maréchal and Preller on this score is rooted in their disagreement as to the status of the "principle of intelligibility."

Preller correctly affirms that the principle of intelligibility, which describes the intellect's persistent and ineradicable desire for more and more sufficient explanations of reality, lies at the heart of Aquinas's epistemology and motivates the celebrated *Quinque Viae* of his natural theology.

> Aquinas evidently believes that the natural desire of the intellect for complete intelligibility cannot be satisfied by anything other than God. That is the probable root cause of his willingness to accept *any* historical argument for the existence of God based on contingent or empirical matters of fact—they manifest the created tendency of the intellect to seek after God.[28]

Preller is unwilling to grant, however, that this human desire to seek ever wider contexts of intelligibility represents more than a psychological necessity governing the way we confront reality. We may be psychologically compelled to think and act *as if* our quest for intelligibility is not ultimately in vain, but, writes Preller, "it does not follow . . . that our desire to 'see the necessity' for the existence of things is more than a psychological ideal doomed to frustration by 'the way things are.'"[29] We might, of course, simply decide to take the natural desire of the mind embodied in the principle of intelligibility as indicative of the actual nature of reality, and proceed accordingly. We might also, in Kantian fashion, conclude that the "practical" benefits derived from such a decision offer sufficient warrant for its rationality. But Preller warns us:

> The point is . . . that such a "taking" is not forced on us; it would be a *decision*. We are free to argue that our natural desire to see the necessity for the existence of things is somehow indicative of how things are, but the presupposition that no natural desire is in vain is not self-evidently true. To elevate such a hypothesis to the level of a synthetic *a priori* of our conceptual system seems a bit rash.[30]

What can we make of this contention that the principle of intelligibility (or sufficient reason) is psychologically, but not logically, necessary? This claim would appear to rest on two assumptions: (1) some aspect of "being" may in principle be unintelligible and (2) since we do not now comprehend the totality of being (the universe in all its complexities), we cannot a priori discount the possibility that it is, in itself, unintelligible. Let us scrutinize the coherence of these assumptions by asking ourselves the question: What do we mean by the "universe?" Surely it can signify nothing other than an organic whole, in which each individual element exists in a complex yet intimate relationship with all other elements. From this understanding flow two important corollaries: (1) there can be no isolated elements in the universe; and (2) no element of the universe can be completely understood unless viewed against the background of the totality. Hence, there can be no mere "matters of fact" or "brute givens" if, by that, one means elements of the universe whose sufficient explanation is not inextricably intertwined with the evolution of the totality. Consequently, one can only speak of the possible existence of elements of the universe that are in principle unintelligible if one's reckonings are beclouded by a faulty grasp of the nature of things. Furthermore, if no part of the whole that is the universe can be in principle unintelligible, then the possibility of the unintelligibility of the whole (the totality of the parts) is ruled out as well.

The argument here is that the universe must be understood as a coherent whole, and thus must be intelligible, in itself (*quoad se*): something cannot "be" and not "be intelligible" at the same time. To entertain the possibility that any event in the universe could be *inherently* unintelligible (that it could *just* occur without an antecedent cause) is to involve oneself in the absurd assertion that "being" can emanate from "nonbeing."

However, Maréchal's commitment to realism and to the universe's intrinsic intelligibility does not necessarily imply that the universe in all its complexity must be completely accessible to unaided finite minds such as ours (*intelligible quoad nos*).[31] In line with Aquinas, Maréchal holds that the satisfaction of our intellectual longing, our quest for the absolute, can only be achieved through the intervention of God's grace. But, even if we set aside this presupposition, and assert that the chances of the unaided human intellect's attaining its final end cannot be determined in advance, Maréchal's analysis is not thereby undermined. The validity of his realist epistemology rests on his demonstration of two vital conclusions: (1) the quest for total understanding is the lifeblood of all cognitive striving; and (2) the principle of intelligibility is not only a psychological imperative of human reason, but an ontologically necessary feature of the universe, as such.[32]

Some, like Preller, might still want to maintain that we cannot be sure that the universe, as such, is not a mere matter of fact: a reality whose existence simply defies explanation. Here, we must be clear about the precise distinction between "finite" and "infinite" being. The ultimate mark of finite being is that its existence is merely contingent or possible. That which is contingent or possible can never, *on its own*, become actual. To assert that it can bespeaks a fundamental misunderstanding of the very meaning of contingency and possibility. It is to claim that the contingent is the necessary, and that the possible is the actual. In short, the series of finite elements that make up the universe cannot be the ground or sufficient condition of the universe's own being or existence. Hence, to speak of the finite without simultaneously recognizing the existence of the infinite as its necessary precondition is to talk literal nonsense.

Due to his confusion on this issue, Preller concludes that Aquinas, therefore also Maréchal, comes to the existence of the absolute as a logically necessary condition of our intellectual activity, by the unwarranted injection of a theological assumption into a purportedly philosophical analysis. In Preller's view, Aquinas knows on the basis of *revelation* that the created human intellect is oriented towards its creator as its final end and fulfillment. It is this prior theological perspective that leads thinkers like Aquinas and Maréchal to construe the essentially ambiguous activity of the intellect as necessarily revealing a teleological orientation toward an actually existing absolute being.[33]

Unlike Preller, Maréchal is not prepared to dismiss summarily the Scholastic axiom "a natural desire cannot be in vain" (*desiderium naturae non potest esse inane*); but neither does he assume its universal acceptance in all philosophical schools, and thus, he does not base his affirmation of the absolute being, as the final end of our intellectual striving, upon it. Still less would Maréchal accept Preller's contention that philosophical and theological analyses are so uncritically interwoven in Aquinas's epistemology. For his own part, Maréchal roundly rejects the "fideist escape," which seeks to solve philosophical problems with theological arguments.

Maréchal has tried to demonstrate that the dynamism of the intellect, as an a priori condition for the possibility of any object of consciousness, is a fundamental drive underlying all mental operations; it is a necessary condition for the power of conceptualization that is the hallmark of our human confrontation with the world. Maréchal has further tried to show that this dynamism coincides with the affirmation of the absolute being as the ultimate *terminus ad quem* of intellectual striving. All other cognitive operations must be seen as essentially subordinate moments in this overarching quest for total intelligibility or assimilation with the absolute. Joseph Donceel accurately mirrors the mind of Maréchal on this central issue when he writes:

> We would have no concepts, no ideas, we would be unable to think and to speak, we would have neither language nor civilization, we would be confined to the animal level of knowing, were it not for the fact that whatever we know is known by us against the Infinite Horizon of Being, of God. Hence the intending of this horizon, the (implicit) affirmation of God, is the *a priori* condition of the possibility of all human thought and action. It is not only psychologically necessary for humans to affirm God's existence . . . it is also logically necessary.[34]

In Maréchal's analysis, the principle of intelligibility requires that we understand the intellect as a power of dynamic striving which implicitly affirms the necessary existence of the absolute being in all its operations. Our thought is not adrift; it has a direction (*telos*). It is, by its very nature, necessarily oriented toward the fullness of being.

Maréchal and Contemporary Epistemology

By way of critique, Preller also raises the logical possibility of alternative conceptual schemes that could radically transform our interpretation of experience.

Reality is *entirely* reconceivable. Not only the intelligible forms of substances (defined in terms of sensible properties) but also the intentional forms of sensible qualities result from the conceptual powers of the intellect and not from what is merely given in experience. Our experience of the accidents of objects has no more direct claim to being veridical than our judgments about the nature of things.[35]

Preller is here enunciating the doctrine of cognitive relativism; namely, truth is relative to conceptual schemes that may be incommensurable with one another. Since this doctrine and a cluster of related issues are at the heart of current debate in epistemology, I would like to deal with them at some length by comparing Maréchal's perspectives with those gleaned from some prominent contemporary epistemological theorists. Even a partial list of the factors contributing to the genesis of this epistemological doctrine would be impressive: the rise of historical consciousness and its assertion of the historically conditioned nature of all worldviews, the emphasis in the sociology of knowledge on the socially conditioned nature of all visions of reality, the contention in the philosophy of science that all scientific observation and appraisal is ineluctably theory-laden, as well as the hermeneutics of suspicion as practiced by Nietzsche, Marx, and Freud, whose numerous disciples now wield considerable influence in academic departments, with a mission to "deconstruct" vast tracts of our tradition.

Without denying the significance of these and other possible factors in the evolution of cognitive relativism, I would argue that we can best attain a proper grasp of its apparent plausibility if we unearth its foundation in a relativist reading of Kant; in particular, of his basic distinction between our mode of conceiving reality and reality-in-itself (*Ding an sich*). In Kant's view, we can only know the appearance of reality as filtered through our conceptual scheme; thus, the thing-in-itself—reality in its pure nature or aseity—is opaque and impenetrable. For Kant, however, there was only one conceptual scheme; namely, the scheme structured by the presuppositions of Euclidean geometry and Newtonian physics. Kant believed that one of his great contributions to our theoretical life was to demonstrate that this scheme was coterminous with the powers of human conceptualization as such.

It is precisely the assertion concerning the uniformity of human conceptual powers that the doctrine of cognitive relativism calls into question. Kant was certainly correct in pointing out the role of the "subject" in the construction of human experience, but the proponents of incommensurability balk at the claim that there is only one human conceptual scheme. Haven't the developments since Kant in mathematics, physics, and the social sciences demonstrated the rich and diverse nature of human conceptualizing and, consequently, the parochiality of Kant's view? Must we not recognize a multiplicity of conceptual schemes, each with its own distinctive historically and culturally conditioned appropriation of the mysterious *Ding an sich* that continually confronts us? Since the thing-in-itself is unavailable to us as an absolute benchmark by which to evaluate the veracity of contending conceptual schemes, what remains at our disposal—so the argument goes—is cognitive relativism.

The relativist reading of Kant is much in vogue these days in philosophical circles, but there are still some contrary voices. I would like to join their insights with those of Maréchal in a critique of the very possibility of cognitive relativism.

Going to the root of the matter, I would question the very possibility of alternative conceptual schemes as portrayed by cognitive relativists. Such thinkers lay great emphasis on the fact that there are, and have been, numerous different systems by which the same external reality has been interpreted and explained. One can cite as examples the magical systems of our primitive ancestors or the Ptolemaic, Aristotelian, Euclidean, Newtonian, and Einsteinian theories as to the nature of things. But experience teaches us that such admittedly different theoretical approaches to reality do not actually represent alternative conceptual schemes. If they did, how could communication be possible among them? The fact is that the entire hermeneutic enterprise requires some matrix of intellectual commonality that cuts across the boundaries of divergent intellectual systems. More than two centuries ago Giambattista Vico recognized this fact: "There must be in the nature of human institutions a mental language common to all nations, which uniformly grasps the substance of things feasible in human social life and expresses it with as many diverse modifications as these same things may have diverse aspects."[36]

Centuries earlier, the Scholastics sought to account for the intertranslatability of the world's languages by making a distinction between the *terminus conceptus* (concept) and the *terminus prolatus* (spoken or written world). Although words for external objects might differ, in the Scholastics' reckoning, there must be be commonality at the conceptual level as a necessary condition for the evident success of translation and cross-cultural communication.

In responding to arguments like these, Richard Rorty grants that "incommensurable" is too strong an adjective to describe the differences that exist among divergent historical or contemporary interpretive systems. Nevertheless, he contends that, by extrapolating from such differences, we can imagine some galactic civilization of the future whose view of reality would be so radically different as to be truly incommensurable with our own, and thus represent a genuine alternative conceptual scheme.[37]

By way of counterargument I would point out, with Donald Davidson, that we could never *know* that such an alternative conceptual scheme existed, since any knowledge we could have of it, no matter how fragmentary, would presuppose that we shared something in common with its framers; hence, their scheme would not be truly incommensurable with our own, and thus not genuinely "alternative." To quote Davidson:

> We must conclude, I think, that the attempt to give solid meaning to the idea of conceptual relativism, and hence the idea of a conceptual scheme, fares no better when based on partial failure of translation than when based on total failure. Given the underlying methodology of interpretation, we could not be in a position to judge that others had concepts or beliefs radically different from our own.[38]

Driven by our desire to know, human beings have fashioned numerous ways to understand the universe that envelops them. The intellectual motivation for moving from one theory to another, say, from a Newtonian to an Einsteinian vision, is to achieve a fuller comprehension of the totality of interlocking events that constitute the universe. All intelligent beings would have to operate in the same fashion, for the drive to fathom the mystery of the universe is the essence of intelligence. Thus, the difference that could exist between our intellectual abilities and those of extraterrestrial intelligent creatures, or between our current theories and some grand galactic megatheory of the future, could only be a relative matter of degree, not a radical difference in kind; our differently developed levels of science would simply yield more or less expansive understandings of our common universe.

In short, we cannot coherently conceive of an alternative conceptual scheme in which the principle of intelligibility would not be operative. We can consider the attempts at explanation by our most primitive ancestors or by the inhabitants of Rorty's future galactic civilization, which may differ as much as imaginably possible from our contemporary scientific reckonings, but we cannot conjure up an example of intelligent beings whose intellectual functioning was not governed by a desire to know the universe in an ever more expanding fashion. Such creatures would be like the subhuman species of our current acquaintance, who are entirely immersed in their surroundings through their sense faculties, but who do not possess the capacity for an intellectual grasp of themselves or their environment.

In a related context, Richard Bernstein attempts to uncover a commitment to enhance "freedom" and "openness" in the human conversation as the common moral drive behind the iconoclastic projects of practitioners of radical hermeneutics such as Jacques Derrida and Richard Rorty.[39] In his view, the charges of irrationalism and relativism that have been lodged against them are misdirected; he claims to find, beneath their surface rhetoric, a reasoned protest against our tenacious tendency to absolutize our beliefs and practices, a tendency that inhibits rather than promotes genuine dialogue. For this service, Bernstein believes they are to be lauded for "the moral task of the philosopher or the cultural critic is to defend the openness of the human conversation against those temptations and real threats that seek closure."[40] Similarly, John Caputo says of Derrida and Heidegger:

> Derrida's deconstructive work issues in a grammatological exuberance which celebrates diversity, repetition, alteration. Heidegger's deconstructive work issues in a meditative stillness, which could not be more alert to the play in which all things are swept, but it is

stunned by the power of its sweep and culminates in a deep sense of play in which mortals play out their allotted time.[41]

Seen in the irenic light of these commentators' analysis, the proclamations of radical or deconstructionist hermeneutics appear much tamer than at first glance. In fact, from the Maréchalian perspective, one could partially endorse them as a welcome—albeit rather melodramatic—antidote to the surfeit of reductionism, scientism, or verificationism that has for too long dominated philosophical debate.

Throughout *Radical Hermeneutics* Caputo calls for an openness to the uncanny "play" or "flux" from which the workings of the universe purportedly emanate, and which rigidifying epistemological schemes seek to mask. Such metaphors can be useful if they recall to mind the complexity of the universe we seek to know, and aid us in seeing that the search for truth is not to be narrowly conceived as an algorithmic, unidimensional process, after the fashion, say, of the logical positivists. But liberation from the dogmatisms that shackled human inquiry does not imply that we can now proceed in any way we choose; nor does the demise of a simplistic conception of the rational order governing the universe (the mechanistic model) imply that the universe is arbitrary and capricious, with no rational order to be found. We can readily agree that, "philosophically," our only source of guidance resides in human creativity and resourcefulness, not in some indubitable Cartesian point of departure, without dismissing the need to uncover the principles or structures underlying these capacities. If we dispense with the principle of inference, the principle of noncontradiction and, above all, the principle of intelligibility or sufficient reason as criteria of intelligent human argument, then how are we to distinguish "sense" from "nonsense," meaningful statements from incoherent ravings?

At this point it would be well to relate the thought of Maréchal to another popular current in contemporary epistemological speculation. Hilary Putnam and Joseph Margolis believe they have fashioned an acceptable halfway house between realism and relativism; namely, pragmatic or internal realism. They both accept the Kantian claim that, in the absence of direct intellectual intuition (*intellektuelle Anschauung*), we have no access to reality-in-itself, independent of our conceptual scheme or historically conditioned situation. In Putnam's words:

> How can we pick out any *one* correspondence between our words (or thoughts) and the supposed mind-independent things *if we have no direct access to the mind-independent things?* ... In short, if the mind does not have the ability to grasp external things or forms directly, then no *mental* act can give it the ability to single out a correspondence (or anything else external, for that matter).[42]

To Putnam and Margolis, the search of classical realism for a correspondence between the mind and reality, as such, is no more than an illusory enterprise. But this does not lead them, as one might suspect, into the relativist camp; in fact, they marshall impressive arguments against the tenability of a consistent relativist position. As Margolis writes, for the pragmatic realist,

> the search for the universal foundations of knowledge goes on as before: but that search is now seen to take the form of inspecting alternative, diachronically conservative, general regularities or conditions that, by arguments to the best explanations (themselves alternatively persuasive in accord with different weightings of pertinent considerations), are historically judged to be among the best candidates that have as yet been found for such status.[43]

Two points need to be made here. First, Maréchal is not defending a brand of Platonic realism based on direct intellectual intuition. He is arguing against Kant—and, by extension, against Putnam and Margolis—that we make contact with reality, as it is in itself, through our normal discursive mode of reasoning. The contrary claim, made by Kant and those still under his sway, is rooted in a Platonic prejudice in favor of intuition that unwarrantedly portrays our sense-dependent brand of knowledge as distortive in character.

Second, once we abandon the Kantian phenomenon-noumenon (*Erscheinung-Ding an sich*) distinction, we can correctly construe cognition as the ongoing effort to transcend partial insights into the nature of reality in our quest for complete understanding. And once we realize the "conditioned" nature of our views (by historical circumstances, economic class, reigning scientific paradigm, etc.), intellectual honesty demands that we seek to transcend the limitations such conditions impose upon us. To do otherwise is to wallow in ideology, not to search for truth.

No doubt the naturalism Putnam and Margolis share would make them uneasy with Maréchal's basic epistemological tenet: that the dynamism toward the absolute must be seen as the fundamental animating force of our cognitive operations. Nonetheless, it would seem that Maréchal offers a more accurate analysis of the ineradicable human longing for more comprehensive knowledge than the warmed-over Kantianism on which Putnam and Margolis rely. In short, there is no halfway house between Aristotelian-Thomistic realism and relativism. The *tertium quid* which Putnam and Margolis struggle to enunciate only draws its apparent plausibility from their prior portrayal of full-bodied realism in Platonic terms.

To reiterate, we can only extricate ourselves from the web of cognitive relativism if we give up the specious Kantian distinction between reality-in-itself and the mere appearance of reality to us, which implies that the purported knower is forever barred from any genuine knowledge of the nature of things. As we have seen, it is a central goal of Maréchal's intellectual mission to encourage us precisely in this direction. He sets out to demonstrate the necessity of objective affirmation, whether we begin with the ontological approach to knowledge of ancient and medieval philosophy, or engage in a transcendental approach in the fashion of modern philosophy. We must come to realize that our concepts are not closed in on themselves but have an "objective reference": in scholastic parlance, our concepts are the means (*id quo*) by which we know reality directly and not, themselves, the object of knowledge (*id quod intelligitur*). Hence, our conceptual efforts put us in direct contact with reality, the fathoming of which, under the inexorable impulse of our drive toward the absolute, constitutes the essence of cognitive growth and development. In this regard, Maréchal's voice can be joined with that of Donald Davidson, who exhorts us to abandon the cognitively stultifying dogma of conceptual schemes.

> In giving up dependence on the concept of an uninterpreted reality, something outside all schemes and science, we do not relinquish

the notion of objective truth—quite the contrary. Given the dogma of a dualism of scheme and reality, we get conceptual relativity, and truth relative to a scheme. Without the dogma, this kind of relativity goes by the board. Of course truth of sentences remains relative to language, but that is as objective as can be. In giving up the dualism of scheme and world, we do not give up the world, but reestablish unmediated touch with the familiar objects whose antics make our sentences and opinions true or false.[44]

But how can we explain that, despite the arguments we have put forth in defense of realism, a contemporary thinker might still cling to anti-realism (we can never be completely certain that our understanding of reality corresponds to the way things actually are)? Maréchal's response to this question is most instructive:

> Because [the anti-realist] wishes to reach, instead of the undeniable, objective but indirect evidence of the affirmation, the objective direct evidence of ontological intuition . . . he believes that he can know things rationally only by directly penetrating into their essence. . . . If this chimerical wish of knowing in a purely intuitive way were fulfilled, there would be no more need for a critique of knowledge. Thus, strangely enough, a hypercritique leading into absolute relativism turns into the worst metaphysical dogmatism. It posits arbitrarily as an unsatisfied methodological exigency what ontologism, in an equally arbitrary way, posited as a necessary mode of our understanding. Ultimately, absolute relativism is nothing but disappointed inverse rationalism.[45]

Maréchal is here anticipating a central theme that pervades Bernard Lonergan's brilliant work on cognitional theory in books such as *Insight* and *Method in Theology*. He is alluding to the fact that Kant's critique of theoretical reason, and the various forms of contemporary relativism that are directly or indirectly under its influence, remain uncritical heirs of the Platonic doctrine of direct intellectual intuition. As a result, the products of the discursive (indirect) mode of our intellectual operations are relegated to the realm of "appearances" or "perspectives," which somehow always miss the ever-illusive core of reality. The deleterious effects of this doctrine on our theory of knowledge can only be overcome by outgrowing the naive assumption that cognition consists in an intuitive "look" at what is out there to be known. Rather, cognition is a process by which our sense experience is transformed into "knowledge" by our conceptual capacities under the guidance of the first principles. In other words, knowledge of the "real" world is a result of a patient, persistent, intelligent, and rational appropriation of what is sensibly given. Furthermore, our metaphysical doctrines (essence or form as the *fundamentum in re* of our universal concepts, the immaterial capacity of the mind that complements sense perception, and ultimately the very doctrine of God) are necessary conclusions we derive not from direct intuitive insight, but by reflection on the activity of the knowing subject as it encounters the world.

What Maréchal offers us is not a finished system but a way of looking at the history of Western philosophy that unmasks the inadequacies and distortions of rationalist and empiricist epistemology, and that engenders a profound respect for the wisdom, clarity, and timeliness of Aristotle's and Aquinas's epistemological insights. He shows us that, through a proper understanding of the Aristotelian-Thomistic account of cognition, we can take a critically realist stance in epistemology and thereby circumvent such philosophical impasses as absolutism and relativism, idealism and skepticism. In the end, Maréchal teaches us that our quest for an adequate metaphysical vision of reality is necessarily ongoing, unfinished, and self-correcting, for it has as its goal nothing less than the grasp of God. It is, in its deepest and most fundamental sense, a quest for the absolute.

Notes

Works cited in the notes are generally identified by short titles; if frequently cited, by the following abbreviations:

MJM   Joseph Maréchal. *Mélanges Joseph Maréchal*. 2 vols. Paris: Desclée de Brouwer, 1950.
MR   Joseph Donceel, ed. & trans. *A Maréchal Reader*. New York: Herder & Herder, 1970.
PDD   Joseph Maréchal. *Le Point de Départ de la Méta-physique.* 5 vols. Paris: Desclée de Brouwer, 1964.
ST   Thomas Aquinas. *Summa Theologica*. In Anton C. Pegis, ed. *Basic Writings of St. Thomas Aquinas*. New York: Random House, 1945.

Introduction

1. Gerald A. McCool, *Catholic Theology in the Nineteenth Century*, 138.
2. Ibid., 3.

Chapter 1. The Rise and Fall of the Aristotelian-Thomistic Synthesis

This chapter contains material that previously appeared in my "Scotus and Ockham: A Dialogue on Universals," *Franciscan Studies* 45 (1985):83–96.

1. *PDD* 1:11. Where I do not indicate Donceel's translation (*MR*), the translation is my own. Likewise, with all other non-English sources: where I do not indicate a standard translation, I have provided my own.
2. *MR*, 4; *PDD* 1:11.
3. For an excellent discussion of Kleutgen's work, see Gerald A. McCool, *Catholic Theology.*
4. *MR*, 5; *PDD* 1:13.
5. *MR*, 5; *PDD* 1:13–14.
6. *PDD* 1:19.

7. For Aristotle's treatment, see *Metaphysics* IV, 3 & 4; especially 1005a & 1005b.

8. *PDD* 1:25.

9. Ibid.

10. Ibid., 47.

11. In this regard, Michael Polanyi affirms: "Since the sceptic does not consider it rational to doubt what he himself believes, the advocacy of 'rational doubt' is merely the sceptic's way of advocating his own beliefs." *Personal Knowledge*, 297.

12. As quoted in *MR*, 9; *PDD* 1:49.

13. *PDD* 1:63–64.

14. Ibid., 74.

15. Ibid.

16. Ibid., 75.

17. Ibid., 76.

18. Ibid., 74.

19. Ibid.

20. Bernard J. F. Lonergan, *Insight*, 412.

21. Ibid., 357.

22. *MR*, 10; *PDD* 1:87.

23. "Parmenides," Fragment 8, 1. 26ff, in G. S. Kirk & J. E. Raven, *The Pre-Socratic Philosophers* (Cambridge: Cambridge University Press, 1963), 276.

24. See Aristotle's *Physics* I, 7 and *Metaphysics* IX, 8.

25. See Aristotle's *Physics* II, 8.

26. *PDD* 1:82.

27. Aristotle, *Metaphysics* XII, 4 & 5.

28. Marjorie Grene, *The Knower and the Known*, 63.

29. *PDD* 1:84–85.

30. Ibid., 97–98.

31. Thomas Aquinas, *ST* I, 85, 1. I am employing the English Dominican translation of this and other cited works by Aquinas, as contained in Anton C. Pegis, ed., *Basic Writings of St. Thomas Aquinas*.

32. *PDD* 1:104.

33. Aquinas, *ST* I, 85, 1, Respondeo.

34. Our claim is that critical realists like Aristotle and Aquinas employ a kind of transcendental reasoning in their attempt to describe the metaphysical structures that account for order and intelligibility of the physical universe. D. W. Hamlyn thus argues: "Aristotle starts from the fact that the language in which we express our judgments about the world involves certain word-world relations." Aristotle then proceeds to "ask what must be the case with regard to the world, or with regard to what there is, if this is to be possible." *Metaphysics*, 5.

35. *PDD* 1:256–57.

36. See Etienne Gilson, *John Duns Scot,* and Frederick C. Copleston, *A History of Philosophy* 2, II, chapters 45–50.

37. *PDD* 1:123–24.

38. Allan B. Wolter, "Duns Scotus," in *Encyclopedia of Philosophy* (New York: Macmillan, 1967) 2:431.

39. John Duns Scotus, *Reportata Parisiensia* I, d. 45, q. 2, n. 9ff; entire text appears in *Opera Omnia* (Paris) vol. 23.

40. See Aquinas, *ST* I, 85, 1.

41. Scotus, *Ordinatio* II, d. 3, q. 1, n. 7; entire text appears in *Opera Omnia* (Civ. Vaticana) vol. 7.

42. *PDD* 1:153.

43. Scotus, *Quaestiones Subtilissimae in Metaphysicam Aristotelis* VII, q. 13, n. 21; entire text appears in *Opera Omnia* (Paris) vol. 7.

44. Ibid., q. 18, n. 8.

45. Ibid.

46. Copleston, *History of Philosophy* 2, II, 238. For a defense of Scotus's doctrine of universals against Ockham's critique, and for an attempt to relate their late medieval dispute to the current philosophical discussion of universals, see my "Scotus and Ockham."

47. Gilson, *Being and Some Philosophers,* 76.

48. *PDD* 1:158.

49. Scotus, *In Metaphysicam* VII, q. 13, n. 23.

50. Scotus, *Reportata Parisiensia* III, d. 14, q. 3, n. 8.

51. Gilson, *Duns Scot,* 550.

52. *PDD* 1:212.

53. Ibid., 219.

54. In William of Ockham's words: "Intuitive cognition is such that when one thing known by means of it inheres as an accident in another, or is locally distant from the other, or stands in some other relation to the other, then non-complex cognition of these things gives us an immediate knowledge whether a certain thing inheres or does not inhere in another, or whether it is distant from it or not, and so for other contingent truth. . . . Generally speaking, any non-complex cognition of one or more terms or things, is an intuitive cognition, if it enables us to know a contingent truth, especially about present facts." Philotheus Boehner, ed. & trans., *William Ockham: Philosophical Writings,* 26.

55. Ernest A. Moody, "William of Ockham," in *Encyclopedia of Philosophy* 8:309.

56. Ockham, *Ordinatio* I, d. 2, q. 6, 172; entire text appears in *Opera Theologica* 2 (St. Bonaventure, N.Y.: Franciscan Institute, 1970).

57. *PDD* 1:227.

58. Boehner, *Ockham: Philosophical Writings*, 36.

59. Ibid., xxvii–xxviii.

60. Gilson describes the heart of Ockham's philosophy as follows: "We know that there are things because we feel them; we know equally that we can use certain images as signs for certain classes of things; we also know that every one of these natural signs stands for a real or possible individual contained within that class; but beyond that we know nothing, and nothing can be known, because the reason things are what they are rests ultimately upon the free will of God." *The Unity of Philosophical Experience*, 78.

61. *PDD* 1:234.

62. Ibid., 248–49.

63. *MR*, 15–16; *PDD* 1:251.

64. Marilyn McCord Adams, *William Ockham* 1:601. In a similar vein, Ernest Moody remarks: "As Hochstetter has so well shown, Ockham's philosophy based itself squarely on the principle of natural causation, and for all its emphasis on the omnipotence of God, it held fast to the scholastic conception of a natural order and of real secondary causes." "Ockham, Buridan, and Nicholas of Autrecourt," in James F. Ross, ed., *Inquiries into Medieval Philosophy*, 303. The textual evidence certainly supports the views of Adams, Moody, and Hochstetter that Ockham cannot be classified as a skeptic as far as his own intentions and explicit comments are concerned. The issue that Maréchal is raising is whether, given Ockham's epistemology, the Venerable Inceptor was consistent in not taking a skeptical position?

65. Moody, "Ockham," 297; and Adams, *Ockham*, 628.

66. John Marenbon, *Later Medieval Philosophy*, 187–88.

67. Moody, "Ockham," 304.

68. Copleston offers what we take to be a balanced assessment of the issue when he writes: "The phrase 'Ockhamist Movement' is perhaps something of a misnomer. For it might be understood as implying that William of Ockham was the sole fountainhead of the 'modern' current of thought in the fourteenth century and that the thinkers of the movement all derived their ideas from him. . . . The names 'nominalism' and 'terminism' were used synonymously to designate the *via moderna*; and the salient characteristic of terminism was the analysis of the function of the term in the proposition, namely the doctrine of *suppositio* or standing-for . . . but it was Ockham who developed the terminist logic in that conceptualist and 'empiricist' direction which we have come to associate with nominalism. One is justified, therefore, in my opinion, in speaking of the 'Ockhamist Movement,' provided that one remembers that the phrase is not meant

to imply that Ockham was the direct source of all the developments of that movement." *History of Philosophy* 3, 1, 134–35.

Chapter 2. The Plight of the Pre-Kantian Philosophy

1. *MR*, 26; *PDD* 2:8–9.
2. *PDD* 2:15.
3. Nicholas of Cusa, *On Learned Ignorance* I, I, 2, as translated by Jasper Hopkins.
4. Ibid., I, III, 10.
5. Ibid., II, III, 111.
6. *PDD* 2:20. Gilson writes that, according to Cusa: "The universal mystery of things is but a concrete expression of the supreme mystery of God." *Philosophical Experience*, 118.
7. Aquinas, *In Librum de Causis*, lec. 6.
8. Strictly speaking, identification in a univocal sense would count as idolatry. Certain conceptions or pure perfections, not necessarily confined to the finite material realm (e.g., goodness and intelligence), could be posited of God by analogy.
9. Aquinas, *De Potentia* 7, 5.
10. Aquinas, *ST* I, 13, 5.
11. Maréchal, "*A propos du sentiment de présence chez les profanes et les mystiques*," in *Etudes sur la Psychologie des Mystiques* (Paris: Desclée de Brouwer, 1938) 1:120–21.
12. Gilson, *Philosophical Experience*, 101–02.
13. *PDD* 2:33–34.
14. Gilson, *Philosophical Experience*, 125.
15. *PDD* 2:44.
16. René Descartes, *Rules for the Direction of the Mind*, II, 366. For Descartes's work, I am using the John Cottingham, Robert Stoothoff, and Dugald Murdoch translations contained in *The Philosophical Writings of Descartes*.
17. Ibid. 3:368.
18. In Descartes's words: "By the term 'thought', I understand everything which we are aware of as happening within us, in so far as we have awareness of it. Hence, *thinking* is to be identified here not merely with understanding, willing and imagining, but also with sensory awareness." *Principles of Philosophy* I, 9, 7.
19. *PDD* 2:54.
20. Ibid., 55.
21. Descartes, *Meditations on First Philosophy* 4:62.
22. *MR*, 27–28.
23. Gilson comments in this regard: "[Malebranche, Spinoza,

and Leibniz] took up the game at exactly the same point where Descartes dropped it, kept the same hand with the same three cards, the mind, matter and God; and as Descartes himself had already played the first two, and failed, they had but one card left; which accounts for the fact that the three of them played the same card. They had to explain everything by God." *Philosophical Experience*, 188.

24. Nicholas Malebranche, *Dialogues on Metaphysics* III, XV. I am employing the Willis Doney translation in *Nicolas Malebranche: Dialogues on Metaphysics*.

25. *PDD* 2:82–83.

26. Descartes, *Meditations* 6:80.

27. In Malebranche's words: "No power, however great we imagine it, can surpass or even equal the power of God. Now, it is a contradiction that God should will the existence of the chair yet not will that it exist somewhere and, by the efficacy of His volition, not put it there, not conserve it there, not create it there. Hence, no power can transport it where God does not transport, nor fix or stop it where God does not stop it, unless it is because God accommodates the efficacy of His action to the inefficacious action of His creatures." *Dialogues* VII, X.

28. *PDD* 2:86.

29. Malebranche, *Dialogues* VI, VIII.

30. *PDD* 2:91.

31. Benedict Spinoza, *On the Improvement of the Understanding* in R. H. M. Elwes, trans., *Chief Works of Benedict de Spinoza* 2:40. All quotes from Spinoza are taken from the Elwes translation.

32. Spinoza, *Ethics* III, 1.

33. Descartes, *Principles of Philosophy* I, 52, 25.

34. *PDD* 2:104.

35. Spinoza, *Ethics* I, prop. XIV.

36. Spinoza actually teaches that God possesses an infinite number of attributes, but only the modes of thought and extension are known to us. *Ethics* I, prop. X. In proper rationalist fashion, Spinoza defines an attribute as "that which the intellect perceives as constituting the essence of a substance." *Ethics* I, def. IV.

37. Spinoza, *Ethics* I, prop. XXIX.

38. *MR*, 30; *PDD* 2:123.

39. Maréchal, *"Au seuil de la métaphysique: Abstraction ou intuition,"* in *MJM* 1:132.

40. Ibid.

41. *MR*, 32; *PDD* 2:125.

42. Bernard Lonergan sounds a similar note when he writes: "There exists a necessary isomorphism between our knowing and its proportionate known. But the parallel is missed by Spinoza's deductivist *ordo idearum est ordo rerum*. The correct locus of the parallel is to

be found in the dynamic structure of our knowing. Inquiry and understanding presuppose and complement experience; reflection and judgment presuppose and complement understanding. But what holds for the activities, also holds for their contents. What is known inasmuch as one is understanding, presupposes and complements what is known by experiencing; and what is known inasmuch as one is affirming, presupposes and complements what is known by understanding." *Insight*, 486.

43. *PDD* 2:130.

44. Leibniz affirms: "It was thus necessary to recall and in a manner to rehabilitate *substantial forms*, which are so much decried to-day, but in a way which makes them intelligible and separates the use which must be made of them from previous abuse." *Exposition and Defence of the New System* in Mary Morris, trans., *Leibniz: Philosophical Writings*, 99. All quotes from Leibniz will be taken from the Morris translation.

45. Namely, a perfectly wise, powerful, and good God chooses the best possible of all worlds.

46. Gottfried Wilhelm Leibniz, *Monadology* 3. According to Leibniz, these monads, as simple substances (i.e., indivisible), must be nonmaterial in nature, and they exist in a harmony pre-established by God. The correspondence between body and soul in human beings is but a particular case of the pre-established harmony that reigns throughout the universe.

47. Ibid., 7.

48. Leibniz, *Principles of Nature and Grace, Founded on Reason*, 5.

49. *PDD* 2:139.

50. John Locke, *An Essay Concerning Human Understanding* (New York: Dover, 1959), Intro., 2.

51. Ibid., Intro., 8.

52. Ibid., II, I, 3.

53. Ibid., II, I, 4.

54. Ibid., II, XII, 1.

55. Ibid.

56. Ibid., II, VIII, 8.

57. Ibid., II, VIII, 15.

58. Ibid., II, VIII, 10.

59. In this regard, Copleston's remarks are instructive: "He [Locke] oscillates, not between two 'views' (since his declared view is that the object of knowledge is ideas), but between two ways of talking, speaking sometimes as though the idea is the *medium quod* of knowledge (his declared view) and sometimes as though it is the *medium quo* of knowledge." *History of Philosophy* 5:116.

60. John Locke, *Essay* IV, II, 14.

61. According to Locke, this resemblance is direct in the case of primary qualities, and indirect in the case of secondary qualities.

62. *PDD* 2:196.

63. *MR*, 48; *PDD* 2:248.

64. Bertrand Russell, *A History of Western Philosophy*, 613.

65. George Berkeley, *Of the Principles of Human Knowledge* I, 4 in T. E. Jessop & A. A. Luce, eds., *The Works of George Berkeley, Bishop of Cloyne*, vol. 2.

66. Ibid., I, 10.

67. *PDD* 2:208.

68. David Hume, *A Treatise of Human Nature* I, I, Sec. I, 1.

69. Ibid., I, I, Sec. I, 7.

70. Ibid., I, III, Sec. V, 84.

71. Hume, *An Enquiry Concerning Human Understanding* (Oxford: Clarendon Press, 1975) IV, I, 22.

72. In Hume's words: "All inferences from experience, therefore, are effects of custom, not of reasoning. . . . Custom, then, is the great guide of human life. . . . Without the influence of custom, we should be entirely ignorant of every matter of fact beyond what is immediately present to the memory and senses." Ibid., V, I, 36.

73. Hume, *Treatise* I, IV, Sec. VI, 252.

74. Ibid.

75. Hume, *Treatise*, Appendix, 635.

76. Ibid., 635–36.

77. Ibid., 636.

78. Hume, *Enquiry* V, I , 38.

79. *MR*, 43; *PDD* 2:242.

80. *PDD* 2:243.

Chapter 3. Kant and the Post-Kantian Idealists

1. *PDD* 3:10–11.

2. Immanuel Kant, *Critique of Pure Reason*, A 1–A 2. I am employing the Norman Kemp Smith translation.

3. Ibid., A 250.

4. In Kant's words: "There can be in us no modes of knowledge, no connection or unity of one mode of knowledge with another, without that unity of consciousness which precedes all data of intuitions, and by relation to which representation of objects is alone possible. This pure original unchangeable consciousness I shall name *transcendental apperception.* . . . The numerical unity of the apperception is thus the *a priori* ground of all concepts." Ibid., A 107.

5. *PDD* 3:218.

6. Kant, *Pure Reason*, A 255.

7. Kant dwells on this point extensively in the preface to the second edition of the *Critique of Pure Reason*. For example, he asserts: "But when all progress in the field of the supersensible has thus been denied to speculative reason, it is still open to us to enquire whether, in the practical knowledge of reason, data may not be found sufficient to determine reason's transcendent concept of the unconditioned, and so to enable us, in accordance with the wish of metaphysics, and by means of knowledge that is possible *a priori*, though only from a practical point of view, to pass beyond the limits of all possible experience. Speculative reason has thus at least made room for such an extension; and if it must at the same time leave it empty, yet none the less we are at liberty, indeed we are summoned, to take occupation of it, if we can, by practical data of reason." *Pure Reason*, B xxi–B xxii. Of course, Kant takes up the task of defending the rationality of practical belief in the existence of God and the soul in the *Critique of Practical Reason*.

8. Kant, *Pure Reason*, Ibid., B xxx.

9. *PDD* 3:214–15.

10. Kant, *Pure Reason*, A 307

11. *PDD* 3:268.

12. Kant, *Critique of Practical Reason*, 348. I am employing the Thomas Kingsmill Abbott translation as contained in the *Great Books of The Western World*, vol. 42.

13. Ibid., 343.

14. Gilson, *Philosophical Experience*, 238.

15. Maréchal, "*Au seuil*," in *MJM* 1:147.

16. Ibid.

17. Ibid., 147–48.

18. Ibid., 148.

19. In volume 4 of *Le Point de Départ*, Maréchal treats only Fichte in a comprehensive manner. Although there are some summary remarks about Schelling and Hegel (pp. 445–53), Maréchal's chief concern is the origin of the transformation of Kantian critical philosophy into idealism that took root in Fichte's thought. Accordingly, in what follows, we will be concerned centrally with Fichte's work, with occasional reference to the thought of the other two great post-Kantian German idealists.

20. *PDD* 4:338.

21. Copleston sounds this important cautionary note in regard to the proper mode of designating the basic metaphysical principle of the post-Kantian idealists: "The word 'subject' is not really appropriate, except as indicating that the ultimate productive principle lies, so to speak, on the side of thought and not on the side of the sensible thing. For the words 'subject' and 'object' are correlative. And the ultimate principle is, considered in itself, without object. It grounds the

subject-object relationship and, in itself, transcends the relationship. It is subject and object in identity, the infinite from which both proceed." *History of Philosophy* 7, 18–19.

22. Johann Gottlieb Fichte, *First Introduction to the Science of Knowledge* 1, 449. The Fichte quotes are taken from Peter Heath & John Lachs, eds. and trans., *Fichte: Science of Knowledge.*

23. Ibid., 1:423.

24. We are here asserting that there was a natural affinity between metaphysical idealism and Romanticism in their common opposition to the spiritually enervating impact of the mechanistic model on Western culture. We are not at all implying that their methods were identical. The Romantics tended to emphasize feeling and spontaneity, and were wont to glorify poetry and mystical intuition as the highroads to insight and truth. Metaphysical idealists, such as Fichte, were more properly concerned with erecting a systematic and coherent philosophical alternative to the sterile reductionism inherent in the mechanistic worldview.

25. *PDD* 4:348.

26. Fichte, *Second Introduction to the Science of Knowledge* 1:463.

27. Ibid. Stressing the dynamic nature of the intelligence that this process of intuition reveals, Fichte writes: "The intellect, for idealism, is an *act*, and absolutely nothing more; we should not even call it an *active* something, for this expression refers to something subsistent in which activity inheres." *First Introduction* 1:440.

28. *PDD* 4:350.

29. Ibid., 5:37–38.

30. William James, *Principles of Psychology* 1:288–89.

31. In Fichte's words: "The self's striving cannot be posited unless a counter-striving of the not-self is posited." *Foundations of the Entire Science of Knowledge (1794)* 1:288.

32. *PDD* 4:443.

33. Ibid.

34. Ibid., 444.

35. Ibid.

36. James D. Collins, *The Existentialists*, 14.

37. *PDD* 4:452.

Chapter 4. Beyond Kant: The Roots of Trancendental Thomism

This chapter is based in part on my "Can Belief in God Be Basic?" *Horizons* 15/2 (1988):262–82.

1. *MR*, 66; *PDD* 5:16.

2. Ibid.

3. *MR*, 70–71; *PDD* 5:51–52.

4. *MR*, 83; *PDD* 5:68.

5. *MR*, 76; *PDD* 5:58.

6. *MR*, 77; *PDD* 5:59.

7. *MR*, 79; *PDD* 5:62.

8. *MR*, 84; *PDD* 5:68.

9. In Aquinas's words: "Those who wish to search for truth without first considering doubt, are like those who don't know where they're going. . . . Because other sciences consider truth from a particular point of view it is proper for them to doubt individual truths: but this science (metaphysics) as it treats of truth in universal terms, so also should it engage in universal doubt." *Commentary On Metaphysics* III, I.

10. *PDD* 5:82–83.

11. *MR*, 90; *PDD* 5:84.

12. Aquinas, *ST* I, 2, 1, 3.

13. *MR*, 90; *PDD* 5:86.

14. One might attempt to circumvent the rigor of Aquinas's argument by adopting an "agnostic" position, neither affirming nor denying the existence of truth. But this move is a mere theoretical fiction, for a totally noncommittal position is not possible in the practical order of everyday existence. Human activity necessarily involves choice, which entails a standard of value; this, in turn, requires—wittingly or unwittingly—a standard of truth.

15. Aquinas, *ST* I, 85, 2.

16. *PDD* 5:91.

17. Aquinas, *ST* I, 84, 7.

18. *MR*, 93; *PDD* 5:93.

19. Lonergan, *Verbum*, 172–73.

20. So-called evolutionary epistemology argues that our knowledge must in some sense reflect reality, otherwise it could not possess the survival value it actually does. However, this survival value necessitates not only that there be a correspondence between thought and external reality, but also that this external reality be stable and orderly in nature. A universe in which chaos truly reigned, wherein one could not count on the fundamental order of self-identity, would be unintelligible and thus unknowable. Hence, the principle of identity, which gives formal expression to the fundamental order and stability which coherent thought demands, must be an expression of the nature of reality as well.

21. Grene, *Knower and Known*, 56.

22. *MR*, 105; *PDD* 5:113.

23. Karl Rahner puts it this way: "For St. Thomas . . . *species*

does not means some kind of 'intentional image,' but is an ontological perfecting of the spirit as a thing which is." *Hearers of the Word*, 42.

24. Aquinas, *ST* I, 87, 1.

25. Aquinas, *Summa Contra Gentiles* II, 98, 17.

26. Aquinas, *ST* I, 14, 1.

27. We, of course, have no startling solution to offer to the age-old problem of the nature of mind. Contemporary materialists would no doubt find Aquinas's view anachronistic in that it appears to posit the unverifiable (by positivist criteria) ghost in the machine. Yet, despite all the advances in the understanding of the neurophysiology of the brain, if the truth be told, materialists are no further along in explaining how, from material processes alone, consciousness emerges than were the ancient Greek atomists. In this context, Michael Polanyi's words, written a few decades ago, still seem apropos: "Our existing knowledge of physics and chemistry can certainly not suffice to account for our experience of active, resourceful living beings, for their activities are often accompanied by conscious efforts and feelings of which our physics and chemistry know nothing." *Personal Knowledge*, 336. What seems to be decisive here is the extent to which one is inextricably married to a naturalist ontology as the sole source from which to draw explanations of our human experience. In this regard, Bernard Lonergan offers the following challenge: "If one finds, with regard to men, that all of one's laws and schemes of sensitive psychology, which pertain to the psychic level, do not account for the intelligible talk that men carry on, one has to go to a still higher level and posit intellectual forms that account for human behavior." *Understanding and Being*, 253. Aquinas belongs to a long line of thinkers, continuing down to our day, who find the materialist goal of reducing mind to matter a futile enterprise, and who therefore find it necessary to postulate multiple levels of being (material and nonmaterial) in human beings to account for the phenomenon of mental life or consciousness.

28. Aquinas, *ST* I, 57, 1.

29. *PDD* 5:188.

30. Aquinas, *ST* I, 85, 1.

31. Rahner, *Spirit in the World*, 136.

32. For a thorough demonstration of the inadequacy of the various types of nominalist accounts of cognition, see D. M. Armstrong, *Nominalism and Realism*, vol. 1.

33. Ibid., 136. For an overview of the arguments of Kripke, Donnellan, and Putnam on the necessity of reopening the discussion on universals, see Stephen P. Schwartz, ed., *Naming, Necessity, and Natural Kinds*.

34. John F. Boler, *Charles Pierce and Scholastic Realism*, 50 n.53

35. Aquinas, *ST* I, 85, 1.

36. *MR*, 140; *PDD* 5:217. In Aquinas's own words: "Our intellect both abstracts the intelligible *species* from the phantasms, in so far as it considers the nature of things universally, and nevertheless understands these natures in the phantasms, since it cannot understand things of which it abstracts the *species* without turning to the phantasms." *ST* I, 85, 1.

37. Aquinas, *De Malo* 16, 8, 3.

38. *MR*, 140; *PDD* 5:219.

39. In Maréchal's words: "Every universalizing abstraction binds a multiplicity to a unity; intellectual abstraction substitutes, with a more or less distinct concept, the unity of a specific nature for the plurality of individuals, the unity of genus for the plurality of species and so forth." *PDD* 52:20. On the infinite thrust of the intellect, Aquinas writes: "Our intellect extends into infinity in knowing. This is shown by the fact that whatever finite quality may be presented, our intellect can think of a greater one." *Contra Gentiles* I, 43, 7.

40. *MR*, 140–41; *PDD* 5:219.

41. On the ultimate end of intellectual striving in the thought of Aquinas, Copleston writes: "Though Aquinas maintained that the primary object of the human mind is the nature of the material thing, he also always held that the mind knows all that it does know as being, and that logically prior to the orientation of the human mind as human towards a particular kind of being there is a natural dynamic impulse of the mind as mind to being as such. In fact, the mind is by its nature oriented, as it were, towards the infinite, which is the ground of the will's orientation towards the infinite good and which ultimately makes metaphysics possible." *Aquinas*, 248.

42. Relying on this aspect of Maréchal's thought, Karl Rahner developed his notion of the *Vorgriff* (pre-concept) of being and its vital role in the process of cognition. "It (*Vorgriff*) is a capacity of dynamic self-movement of the spirit, given *a priori* with human nature, directed toward all possible objects. It is a movement in which the particular object is, as it were, grasped as an individual factor of this movement towards a goal, and so consciously grasped in a pre-view of this absolute breadth of the knowable. Through this pre-concept the particular is always, as it were, recognized under the horizon of the absolute ideal of knowledge. Hence it has always already been set within the conscious sphere of the totality of knowable things. Hence, too, it is always already known as not completely filling up this sphere, that is, as limited. Insofar as it is seen to be limited, the essential definition will be understood in itself as wider, and relatively unlimited—that is, it is abstracted." *Spirit*, 60.

43. As Maréchal puts it: "For the awareness of a limit contains

logically, within the very order where the limit occurs, the knowledge of a further possibility." *MR*, 164; *PDD* 5:378.

44. *MR*, 152; *PDD* 5:313–14.

45. *MR*, 248; "Le dynamisme intellectuel dans la connaissance objective," in *MJM* 1:89.

46. Consider, for example, the comments of David Bohm: "Wholeness is what is real and . . . fragmentation is the response of this whole to man's action, guided by illusory perception, which is shaped by fragmentary thought. . . . So what is needed is for man to give attention to his habit of fragmentary thought, to be aware of it, and thus bring it to an end." *Wholeness and the Implicate Order*, 7.

47. Donceel, *The Searching Mind*, 60.

48. *MR*, 171; *PDD* 5:412.

49. Aquinas, *Contra Gentiles* III, 52, 6. Maréchal comments: "Hence the ultimate perfection of our intellect supposes not only that it be free from all material bonds, it requires also an extrinsic condition, standing above our nature; a divine initiative; an active communication of the absolute Being, whose sovereign independence is incompatible with any obligation towards its creature." *MR*, 172; *PDD* 5:419.

50. *MR*, 173; *PDD* 5:420.

51. Maréchal explicitly rejects such a fideist approach to philosophy: "Should we, however, base our whole objective certitude upon our belief in the supernatural object of our revelation, this would be 'fideism,' not a rational critique." Ibid.

52. Kant, *Pure Reason*, A 326 = B 383.

53. Ibid., A 686 = B 714.

54. Ibid., A 679 = B 707.

55. In Maréchal's words: "Although this end is supernatural, it must, in itself, be possible. Else the basic tendency of our intellectual nature turns into a logical absurdity, the appetite for nothingness." *MR*, 184; *PDD* 5:448.

56. In this context, Donceel argues: "Animals do not perceive objects as objects; they do not know that what they perceive is not-I. They are, as Scheller has put it, 'ecstatically immersed in their environment.' That is why they are so perfectly adapted to it and generally so much at a loss outside of it. But that is also why they do not speak and have no culture." *Searching Mind*, 80.

57. *MR*, 181; *PDD* 5:444.

58. *MR*, 181; *PDD* 5:447.

59. *MR*, 183; *PDD* 5:448.

60. *MR*, 185; *PDD* 5:449–50.

61. *MR*, 185; *PDD* 5:450. Maréchal contends that in this argu-

ment he is echoing Aquinas: "All knowing beings implicitly know God in everything they know." *De Veritate* 22, 2, 1.

62. As Maréchal explains: "For an assimilating faculty, which has to look outside itself for that which fills its need, the first interest lies in the good which fills this need. Hence the first known object can only be the assimilated object, not yet formally the activity itself of the assimilating subject." *MR*, 187; *PDD* 5:453.

63. *MR*, 201–2; *PDD* 5:476.

64. *MR*, 84; *PDD* 5:69.

65. *MR*, 192; *PDD* 5:461–62.

66. Donceel, *Searching Mind*, 69.

67. Ibid., 89–90.

68. Stephen E. Toulmin, *Foresight and Understanding*, 115.

69. *MR*, 191; *PDD* 5:459.

70. Rahner, *Spirit*, 182.

71. *MJM* 12:9–30.

Chapter 5. Critique and Conclusion

A portion of this chapter was previously published in my "Grounding the Human Conversation," *The Thomist* 53/2 (1989):35–58.

1. Gilson, *Thomist Realism and the Critique of Knowledge*, 130–31. The original French title of this work is *Réalisme Thomiste et Critique de la Connaissance* (Paris: J. Vrin, 1939).

2. Otto Muck, *The Transcendental Method*, 209.

3. Maréchal as quoted by Muck, ibid., 212.

4. Gilson sees no middle ground here: "We have now examined several types of critical realism and in each instance have come to the conclusion that the critique of knowledge is essentially incompatible and irreconcilable with metaphysical realism. There is no middle ground. You must either begin as a realist with being, in which case you will have a knowledge of being, or begin as a critical idealist with knowledge, in which case you will never come in contact with being." *Realism and Knowledge*, 149.

5. Muck, *Method*, 213.

6. Walter Brugger captures the underlying élan of Maréchal's efforts when he writes: "In no sense did Maréchal represent the transcendental method as the only possible or justified approach. In his view also, the metaphysical critique of the ancients was the natural procedure whereas the transcendental critique was a methodological artifice which demonstrated that the purely phenomenal standpoint was inherently impossible. Both critiques complemented one another and, when consistently carried through, led to the same result. The

ontological object, which was the concern of the ancient critique, includes the transcendental subject; and the transcendental subject,
which is the focus of the modern critique, requires the ontological object." "Dynamistische Erkenntnistheorie und Gottesbeweis" in *MJM*
2:112–13.

7. R. Heinz, *Französische Kantinterpreten im 20. Jahrhundert*,
39.

8. In Maréchal's words: "There is no middle ground between an
intuitive intellect and a discursive intellect, and it is far too evident,
as Kant himself assumes, that, in the intellectual order, we are not
endowed with intuition. An intellectual intuition cannot suffer error
nor doubt in relation to its object and would have no need of a critique.
Furthermore, intellectual intuition does not tolerate the mode of
knowledge by 'judgments,' *per compositionem et divisionem.*" PDD
5:536.

9. *PDD* 5:542. In a similar vein, Rahner writes: "God is posited,
too, with the same necessity as this pre-concept (*Vorgriff*). He is the
thing of which is affirmed absolute 'having existence.' It is true that
the pre-concept does not present God immediately as object of the intellect, because the pre-concept, as condition for the possibility of objective knowledge, does not present any object at all along with itself."
Hearers, 63.

10. Harald Holz, *Tranzendentalphilosophie und Metaphysik*,
130.

11. *PDD* 4:434. As quoted in Quentin Lauer, *Hegel's Concept of
God*, 247.

12. Lauer, *Concept of God*, 276.

13. Ibid., 256.

14. George Wilhelm Friedrich Hegel, "Lectures on the Proofs of
the Existence of God" in *Lectures on the Philosophy of Religion*,
3:285.

15. Lauer, *Essays In Hegelian Dialectic*, 134–35.

16. For a discussion of the relationship between *mythos* and *lo-
gos*, or theology and philosophy, that seeks to integrate Transcendental Thomist and Hegelian perspectives, see my "Beyond Rationalism
and Romanticism: A Critique of Narrative Theology," *The World & I*
(November 1989):602–19.

17. Hans Küng, *Does God Exist?*, 547.

18. The same charge of dogmatism or fideism (albeit of a rather
sophisticated variety) can be leveled against what are now popularly
designated as "post-modern" or "nonfoundationalist" defenses of the
rationality of belief. For a Maréchalian critique of Alvin Plantinga's
assertion that belief in God can be "basic" to a religious community,

and thus immune from external critique, see my "Can Belief in God Be Basic?" *Horizons* 15/2 (1988):262–82.

19. In Küng's words: "Nihilism is irrefutable. There is no rationally conclusive argument against the possibility of nihilism. It is indeed at least possible that this human life, in the last resort, is meaningless. . . . Nihilism is also unprovable. There is no rational argument for the necessity of accepting nihilism. It is indeed also possible that this human life is not, in the last resort, meaningless." *Does God Exist?*, 423–24.

20. Ibid., 447, 451.

21. John L. Mackie, *The Miracle of Theism*, 250. Practical justifications of philosophical or religious beliefs, without theoretical support, are always open to the objection that they represent a violation of intellectual integrity: wishful thinking, no matter how comforting, must not be permitted to supplant critical appraisal. Hans Albert calls Küng to task on just this issue: "To postulate that which one needs is as unacceptable in the domain of practical reason as it is in the theoretical domain. But our author [Küng] . . . has every reason to come to Kant's aid against his critics in this context; for he will employ this method of postulation [*Postulieren*] in a much more frivolous manner than the sober thinker of Königsberg." *Das Elend der Theologie*, 108.

22. Victor Preller, *Divine Science and the Science of the Mind*.

23. Ibid., 61–62.

24. *MR*, 243; *MJM* 1:156.

25. Preller, *Divine Science*, 73.

26. Polyani, *Personal Knowledge*, 339.

27. Preller, *Divine Science*, 65.

28. Ibid., 164

29. Ibid., 171.

30. Ibid., 164.

31. Thinkers who proclaim the possible unintelligibility of the universe *quoad se* seem bedeviled by a naturalized variant of the fundamental principle of idealism "to be is to be perceived" (*esse est percipi*). An idealist like Bishop Berkeley, who still holds for a divine mind that can perceive those realms of the universe beyond the ken of mere mortals, need have no doubts about the intelligibility of those realms. However, the individual of idealist bent, for whom the existence of such a divine mind has become problematic, is seduced by the force of the initial idealist principle to restrict the realm of the actual and intelligible to what lies within the ambit of human experience. Attempting to counteract the hubris that underlies the contemporary manifestations of idealism, Thomas Nagel pointedly remarks: "Not everything about the universe must lie in the path of our possible

cognitive development or that of our descendants—even if beings like us should exist forever. .... [W]hat there is, or what is the case, does not coincide necessarily with what is a possible object of thought for us. Even if through some miracle we are capable in principle of conceiving everything there is, *that is not what makes is it real.*" (emphasis added) *The View From Nowhere*, 92.

32. This second conclusion should lead one to be critical of quantum theory, now fashionable among physicists, which boldly asserts that the activity of subatomic particles is intrinsically indeterminate; hence, the principle of intelligibility does not have universal application. The fact that the behavior of subatomic particles appears indeterminate when examined by our currently intrusive techniques of measurement (we cannot simultaneously measure their position and velocity) does not entail the leap to the quite radical metaphysical conclusion that matter, at its most basic level, is inherently indeterminate. A limitation in our capacities of measurement at the physical level, even if it should prove insuperable, should not be transformed quite simply into a metaphysical hypothesis about the ultimate nature of reality. On this issue, see Stanley L. Jaki, "Chance or Reality: Interaction in Nature Versus Measurement in Physics" in *Chance or Reality and Other Essays*, 1–21. A similar comment can be made in regard to so-called Chaos Theory. See James Gleick, *Chaos*. A lack of predictability on our part as to the course of future events does not imply that they are, at bottom, unintelligible. Certainly the universe is intensely more complex than Laplace and other proponents of the mechanistic model ever imagined. One can reject their simplistic reductionism, and even admit that our grasp of the future will always be tinged with uncertainty, without illogically jumping to the conclusion that our uncertainty implies that the universe is in some "literal" sense chaotic, and thus unintelligible.

33. Comments Preller: "[Aquinas] knows on the basis of revelation that the mind of man is ordered to God as to One Unknown, and he accepts as revealed truth the statement that man is able, on the basis of reason alone, to reflect on that ordering. He then offers as external and probable evidence of the truth of revelation a philosophical account of the 'first principles' of reason which manifests that ordination of the mind to the First Truth. Whatever interpretation of the status of the 'first principles' might be possible, Aquinas 'knows' that his interpretation is correct." *Divine Science*, 172.

34. Donceel, *Searching Mind*, 82. One might perhaps hear in Maréchal's argument and Donceel's commentary the echo of Descartes's claim in the third Meditation: "I clearly understand that there is more reality in an infinite substance than in a finite one, and hence that my perception of the infinite, that is God, is in some way prior to

my perception of the finite, that is myself. For how could I understand that I doubted or desired—that is, lacked something—and that I was not wholly perfect, unless there were in me some idea of a more perfect being which enabled me to recognize my own defects by comparison." *Meditations* 3:45–46. Like Descartes, Maréchal is asserting that the "finite" can only be recognized, as such, against the background of the infinite. However, Maréchal is not arguing that we possess a "clear and distinct" intuitive idea of God; rather, that transcendental analysis of the process of cognition reveals that the infinite longing of the intellect for the absolute animates all our thinking. We grasp the finite as "finite" precisely because of its inability to satisfy this intellectual longing. Hence, God or the absolute is revealed and affirmed as the ultimate horizon against which all thinking takes place.

35. Preller, *Divine Science*, 69.

36. Giambattista Vico, *The New Science of Giambattista Vico* I, II (Elements), para. 161.

37. In Richard Rorty's words: "We can still see that it is rational to expect that the incommunicably and unintelligibly novel will occur, even though *ex hypothesi* we can neither write nor read a science fiction story that describes Galactic civilization. Here, then, we have a case in which there really is a difference between the *ordo cognoscendi* and the *ordo essendi*, and no verificationist argument can apply. *Consequences of Pragmatism*, 8–9.

38. Donald Davidson, "On the Very Idea of a Conceptual Scheme," in *Inquiries into Truth and Interpretation*, 197. Drawing on Davidson's analysis, A. C. Grayling writes: "The very idea of an alternative scheme depends on a shared range of concepts and these . . . will be central and basic concepts at that. It follows that 'alternative' in 'alternative scheme' can only refer to superstructural rather than basic features, and accordingly that all experience recognizable as such by us has certain basic and pervasive features on which our recognition of that experience as experience turns." *The Refutation of Scepticism*, 90.

39. Richard J. Bernstein, *Beyond Objectivism and Relativism*.

40. Ibid., 205.

41. John D. Caputo, *Radical Hermeneutics*, 206.

42. Hilary Putnam, *Realism and Reason*, 207. See also Putnam's *The Many Faces of Realism*.

43. Joseph Margolis, *Pragmatism without Foundations*, 182.

44. Davidson, *Inquiries*, 198.

45. *MR*, 227–28; *PDD* 5:560. There are, of course, other motivating factors, not the least of which are political in nature. In assessing the relativist elements to be found in the work of Kuhn, Feyerabend,

and Foucault, Hilary Putnam writes: "While Kuhn has increasingly moderated his view, both Feyerabend and Michel Foucault have tended to push it to extremes. Moreover there is something political in their minds: both Feyerabend and Foucault link our present institutionalized criteria of rationality with capitalism, exploitation, and even sexual repression. Clearly there are many divergent reasons why people are attracted to extreme relativism today, the idea that all existing institutions and traditions are bad being one of them." *Realism and Reason*, 198. Putnam's remarks say a great deal about the origin of the heavy doses of cognitive relativism one so often finds today in feminist and other victim-oriented brands of philosophizing. Stanley Rosen sees our contemporary situation as one in which the legitimate Romantic protest against the parochiality of Enlightenment canons of rationality has, indeed, run amok. "The twentieth-century rebellion against *the* scientific truth—and the consequent popularity of doctrines of historicism and linguistic conventionalism . . . is thus a rebellion against truth. Whatever was intended by the leaders of this rebellion, there can be no doubt that the thesis that art is worth more than the truth is the dominant principle of our time. We have protected ourselves against rationalism not by prudent moderation in its use but by a reckless embrace of recklessness, or the rejection of rationalism in favor of the imagination." *Hermeneutics as Politics*, 138.

Select Bibliography

Adams, Marilyn McCord. *William Ockham*. 2 vols. Notre Dame, Ind., University of Notre Dame Press, 1987.

Albert, Hans. *Das Elend der Theologie*. Hamburg: Hoffman & Campe, 1979.

Aquinas, Thomas. *Summa contra Gentiles*. Notre Dame, Ind.: University of Notre Dame Press, 1975.

———. *Summa Theologica*. New York: Benziger, 1947–48.

———. *Truth (De Veritate)*. Chicago: H. Regnery, 1952–54.

Armstrong, D. M. *Nominalism and Realism*. 2 vols. Cambridge: Cambridge University Press, 1978.

Bernstein, Richard J. *Beyond Objectivism and Relativism*. Philadelphia: University of Pennsylvania Press, 1983.

Boehner, Philotheus, ed. *William of Ockham: Philosophical Writings*. New York: Bobbs-Merrill, 1964.

Bohm, David. *Wholeness and the Implicate Order*. Boston: Routledge & Kegan Paul, 1980.

Boler, John F. *Charles Pierce and Scholastic Realism*. Seattle: University of Washington Press, 1963.

Caputo, John D. *Radical Hermeneutics*. Bloomington, Ind.: University of Indiana Press, 1987.

Collins, James D. *The Existentialists*. Chicago: H. Regnery, 1952.

Copleston, Frederick C. *Aquinas*. London: Penguin Books, 1957.

———. *A History of Philosophy*. 8 vols. Garden City, N.Y.: Image Books, 1962.

Cottingham, John, et al., trans. *The Philosophical Writings of Descartes*. 2 vols. New York: Cambridge University Press, 1988.

Davidson, Donald. *Inquiries into Truth and Interpretation*. New York: Oxford University Press, 1986.

Donceel, Joseph, ed. *A Maréchal Reader*. New York: Herder & Herder, 1970.

———. *The Searching Mind*. Notre Dame, Ind.: University of Notre Dame Press, 1979.

Doney, Willis, trans. *Nicolas Malebranche: Dialogues on Metaphysics*. New York: Abaris Books, 1980.

Elwes, R. H. M., trans. *The Chief Works of Benedict de Spinoza.* 2 vols. New York: Dover, 1951.

Gilson, Etienne. *Being and Some Philosophers.* Toronto: Pontifical Institute of Medieval Studies, 1952.

———. *Jean Duns Scot.* Paris: J. Vrin, 1952.

———. *The Unity of Philosophical Experience.* London: Sheed & Ward, 1955.

———. *Thomist Realism.* San Francisco: Ignatius Press, 1986.

Gleick, James. *Chaos.* New York: Penguin Books, 1987.

Grayling, Anthony C. *The Refutation of Scepticism.* LaSalle, Ill.: Open Court, 1985.

Grene, Majorie. *The Knower and the Known.* London: Faber & Faber, 1966.

Hamlyn, D. W. *Metaphysics.* Cambridge: Cambridge University Press, 1987.

Heath, Peter & John Lache, eds. & trans. *Fichte: Science of Knowledge.* New York: Meredith Corporation, 1970.

Hegel, Georg Wilhelm Friedrich. *Lectures on the Philosophy of Religion.* New York: Humanities Press, 1968.

Heinz, R. *Französische Kantinterpretation im 20. Jahrhundert.* Bonn: Bouvier, 1966.

Holz, Harald. *Tranzendentalphilosophie und Metaphysik.* Mainz: Matthias-Grünewald, 1966.

Hopkins, Jasper, trans. *Nicholas of Cusa on Learned Ignorance.* Minneapolis: Arthur J. Banning Press, 1981.

Hume, David. *A Treatise of Human Nature.* Oxford: Clarendon Press, 1964.

———. *Enquiry Concerning Human Understanding.* Oxford: Clarendon Press, 1975.

Jaki, Stanley L. *Chance or Reality and Other Essays.* Latham, Md.: University Press of America, 1986.

James, William. *Principles of Psychology.* New York: Henry Holt, 1950.

Jessop, T. E., & A. A. Luce, eds. *The Works of George Berkeley, Bishop of Cloyne.* Vol. 2. New York: Thomas Nelson & Sons, 1949.

Kant, Immanuel. *Critique of Practical Reason* in *Great Books of the Western World* Vol. 42. Chicago: Encyclopaedia Britannica, 1980.

———. *Critique of Pure Reason.* London: Macmillan, 1958.

Küng, Hans. *Does God Exist?* New York: Vintage Books, 1981.

Lauer, Quentin. *Essays in Hegelian Dialectic.* New York: Fordham University Press, 1977.

————. *Hegel's Concept of God*. Albany: State University of New York Press, 1982.

Locke, John. *A Treatise on Human Nature*. Oxford: Clarendon Press, 1985.

Lonergan, Bernard. *Insight*. New York: Longman, 1957.

————. *Understanding and Being*. New York: The Edwin Mellen Press, 1980.

————. *Verbum*. Notre Dame, Ind.: University of Notre Dame Press, 1967.

Mackie, John L. *The Miracle of Theism*. Oxford: Clarendon Press, 1982.

Maréchal, Joseph. *Le Point de Départ de la Métaphysique*. 5 vols. Paris: Desclée de Brouwer, 1964.

————. *Mélanges Joseph Maréchal*. 2 vols. Paris: Desclée de Brouwer, 1950.

————. *Studies in the Psychology of the Mystics*. Albany: Magi Books, 1964.

Marenbon, John. *Later Medieval Philosophy*. New York: Routledge & Kegan Paul, 1987.

Margolis, Joseph. *Pragmatism Without Foundations*. Cambridge, Mass.: Basil Blackwell, 1986.

McCool, Gerald A. *Catholic Theology in the Nineteenth Century*. New York: Seabury Press, 1977.

McKeon, Richard P., ed. *The Basic Works of Aristotle*. New York: Random House, 1968.

Morris, Mary, trans. *Leibniz: Philosophical Writings*. New York: Dutton 1965.

Muck, Otto. *The Transcendental Method*. New York: Herder & Herder, 1968.

Nagel, Thomas. *The View from Nowhere*. New York: Oxford University Press, 1986.

Ockham, William. *Opera Theologica*. St. Bonaventure, N.Y.: Franciscan Institute, 1967–84.

Pegis, Aton, ed. *Basic Writings of St. Thomas Aquinas*. New York: Random House, 1945.

Polanyi, Michael. *Personal Knowledge*. New York: Harper & Row, 1962.

Preller, Victor. *Divine Science and the Science of God*. Princeton: Princeton University Press, 1967.

Putnam, Hilary. *Realism and Reason*. New York: Cambridge University Press, 1987.

————. *The Many Faces of Realism*. LaSalle, Ill.: Open Court, 1989.

Rahner, Karl. *Hearers of the Word.* New York: Herder & Herder, 1969.
————. *Spirit in the World.* New York: Herder & Herder, 1968.
Rorty, Richard. *Consequences of Pragmatism.* Minneapolis: University of Minnesota Press, 1982.
Rosen, Stanley. *Hermeneutics as Politics.* New York: Oxford University Press, 1987.
Ross, James F., ed. *Inquiries into Medieval Philosophy.* Westport, Conn.: Greenwood Press, 1971.
Russell, Bertrand. *A History of Western Philosophy.* New York: Simon & Schuster, 1945.
Schwartz, Stephen, ed. *Naming, Necessity, and Natural Kinds.* Ithaca, N.Y.: Cornell University Press, 1977.
Scotus, John Duns. *Opera Omnia.* Civitas Vaticana: Typis Polyglottis Vaticanis, 1950-.
————. *Opera Omnia.* Paris: Vives, 1891–95.
Thomas, George F. *Religious Philosophies of the West.* New York: Charles Scribner's Sons, 1965.
Toulmin, Stephen E. *Foresight and Understanding.* New York: Harper & Row, 1963.
Van Riet, Georges. *Thomistic Epistemology.* St. Louis: Herder & Herder, 1963.
Vico, Giambattista. *The New Science of Giambattista Vico.* Garden City, N.Y.: Doubleday, 1961.
Wolter, Allan B., ed. & trans. *John Duns Scotus: Philosophical Writings.* New York: Bobbs-Merrill, 1962.

Index

Dogmatism, 77, 126, 160n.18
Donceel, Joseph, 103, 114, 115, 134, 158n.56
Doubt, 155n.9; methodic, 40–41, 89–90
Dualism, Cartesian, 45, 46, 47, 49
Duns Scotus, John, 18, 25; on cognitive process, 23–24; on common nature, 21–22; on formalities, 19–20
Dynamism, 52, 83, 107, 113; and cognition, 108–9, 141; fundamental, 117–18; pure, 78, 80; role of, 88–89

Ego, 78, 79–80, 81. *See also* "Self"
Empiricism, 11, 43, 57; Berkeley's, 58–59; Hume's, 62–63; and rationalism, 64–65; and "self," 61–62
Epistemology, 133, 134, 135, 155n.20; Aristotelian-Thomistic, 85–86, 93–94, 96; Cartesian, 42–43; Malebranchian, 46–47; Thomistic, 129–30
Essay Concerning Human Understanding (Locke), 55
Existence, 6–7, 106
Experience, 9, 65, 77, 86, 136, 152n.72; concepts of, 134–35; sense and, 87, 130–31

Faith, 28, 36–37, 42
Fichte, Johan Gottlieb, 75, 153n.19; on consciousness, 78–79, 80–81; on ego, 79–80; idealism of, 76–77
Fideism, 126, 158n.51, 160n.18
Five Ways (Thomas Aquinas), 36–37

Form, and matter, 9–10, 21
Formalities, 19–20

Gilson, Etienne, 22, 24, 38, 70, 147n.60; on realism, 119–20, 159n.4
God, 160nn.9, 18; affirmation of, 116–17, 134; approaches to, 36–37; as causal agent, 48–49, 148nn.60, 64; and cognition, 114–15; concepts of, 41–42, 44–45, 46, 104–5, 107, 108–9, 122, 123–24, 126, 127, 149nn.8, 23, 27, 36, 158n.61, 162n.34; as transcendent, 51–52
Grace, 38
Greeks, 5
Grene, Marjorie, 14

Haecceitas, 20, 21
Hegel, Georg Wilhelm Friedrich, 76; philosophy of, 123–24, 125–26
Heidegger, Martin, 138
Heinz, R., 122
Heraclitus, 6, 12
Hermeneutics, radical, 138–39
Hume, David, 44, 58, 152n.72; on causality, 60–61; empiricism of, 62–63; on ideas, 59–60; on mind, 61–62; on "self," 78–79

Ideal, and real, 92
Idealism, x, 24, 47, 75, 83, 154n.24; absolute, 82, 122; post-Kantian, 76–77
Ideas, 116; definition of, 59–60; and knowledge, 56–57, 151n.59; simple vs. complex, 55–56
Identity, 6, 8, 13, 86

Scotus, John Duns. *See* Duns
  Scotus, John
"Self," 61, 62, 78–79
Self-assertion, 7–8
Self-concept, 19
Self-consciousness, 53, 66
Sense, 65–66, 71–72, 109, 129
Senses, 60, 130–31; contact of,
  91–92, 95; and intellect, 54–
  55, 95; and knowledge, 11–13
Skepticism, 6, 7–8, 60, 62, 86,
  89–90, 146n.11
Socrates, 9
Sophists, 6, 8–9, 111
Species, 10, 92, 93, 99, 100,
  157n.36
Spinoza, Benedict, 46, 62,
  150nn.36, 42; on integrated
  rationalism, 47–52
Spiritualism, 42

Tathandlung, 78
Teleology, 53
Theory, and reason, 69–71
Thinking, activity of, 103–4
Thomas Aquinas, x, xii, 12, 15,
  18, 21, 24, 89, 91, 111, 134,
  143, 146n.34, 155n.14,
  156n.27, 157n.41; on abstraction, 17, 96, 157n.36; on contemplation of God, 37–38; on
  cognition, 94, 101, 128; on
  doubt, 89–90, 155n.9; on intellect, 95, 104, 129, 130; on
  knowledge, 16, 98–99
Thomism: methodic doubt in,
  89–90; thought in, 81–82. *See*

also Transcendental Thomism
*Thomisme devant la Philoso-
  phie Critique, Le* (Marechal),
  85–86
Thought, xii–xiii, 81–82, 103,
  113, 149n.18, 158n.46; and
  being, 52, 111–12
Toulmin, Stephen, 116
Transcendental analysis, 90, 115,
  121, 146n.34; apperception
  and, 66, 87; critique of, 86–
  87, 159n.6; and dynamism,
  107–8; and God, 51–52;
  Kant's, 75–76, 100, 112, 120
Transcendental Thomism, xi,
  51–52, 83–84, 88, 122, 125–
  26
Truth, 7, 35, 155nn.9, 14,
  162n.33; conceptual schemes
  of, 135, 163n.38

Ultrarealism, 20, 23
Understanding, 74; and reason,
  30, 68–69; and sense, 65–66,
  71–72
Universals, 10–11, 15, 21, 27
Universe, 137; intelligibility of,
  112–13, 126, 132–33, 61n.31;
  as limited, 102–3; unified vision of, 5–6

Vaihinger, Hans, 70

Wittgenstein, Ludwig, 97
Wolter, Allan B., 19
Woodham, Adam, 32
World order, 82